T0305761

Hands-on
Project
Management
Practice your Skills with
Simulation Based Training

Hands-on
Project
Management
Practice your Skills with
Simulation Based Training

Avraham Shtub
Technion Israel Institute of Technology, Israel

Moshe Rosenwein
Columbia University, USA

NEW JERSEY · LONDON · SINGAPORE · BEIJING · SHANGHAI · HONG KONG · TAIPEI · CHENNAI · TOKYO

Published by

World Scientific Publishing Co. Pte. Ltd.

5 Toh Tuck Link, Singapore 596224

USA office: 27 Warren Street, Suite 401-402, Hackensack, NJ 07601

UK office: 57 Shelton Street, Covent Garden, London WC2H 9HE

Library of Congress Cataloging-in-Publication Data
Names: Shtub, Avraham, author. | Rosenwein, Moshe, author.
Title: Hands-on project management : practice your skills with simulation based training /
    Avraham Shtub (Technion Israel Institute of Technology, Israel),
    Moshe Rosenwein (Columbia University, USA).
Description: 1 Edition. | New Jersey : World Scientific, [2018] | Includes bibliographical references.
Identifiers: LCCN 2017045432 | ISBN 9789813200531
Subjects: LCSH: Project management--Study and teaching--Simulation methods. |
    Management--Study and teaching--Simulation methods.
Classification: LCC HD69.P75 S5388 2018 | DDC 658.4/04--dc23
LC record available at https://lccn.loc.gov/2017045432

British Library Cataloguing-in-Publication Data
A catalogue record for this book is available from the British Library.

For any available supplementary material, please visit
http://www.worldscientific.com/worldscibooks/10.1142/10293#t=suppl

Desk Editor: Shreya Gopi

Typeset by Stallion Press
Email: enquiries@stallionpress.com

Printed in Singapore

I dedicate this book to my late parents
Miriam and Henrik Shtub.

Avraham Shtub

I dedicate this book to my children,
David and Danielle, Hannah, and Benjamin.

Moshe Rosenwein

The cover of this book is a picture of the Bahá'í gardens in Haifa, Israel. Nine concentric circles provide the main geometry of the eighteen terraces of this garden. The site is a model known as the Kúh-i-Núr (Mountain of Light), facing and overshadowed by the Daryá-yi-Núr (Ocean of Light).

Our book is based on models (the software, Project Team Builder, models actual and realistic projects). This is the source of the name SandboxModel — the company that created Project Team Builder.

Project Team Builder (PTB), the software that accompanies this book, is web-based.

Using Internet Explorer from a Windows computer, connect to http://www.sandboxmodel.com/book

To use PTB, you must enter the unique access code provided on the inside front cover of this book. (If you are using an e-book, please visit http://www.worldscientific.com/page/10293-info-request for your unique access code.)

This book also has accompanying video tutorials. Visit http://www.sandbox-model.com/content/hands-on-project-management-training-book-videos to access the videos.

Contents

Preface   ix

About the Authors   xiii

Chapter 1   Introduction to Project Management   1

Chapter 2   Introduction to the Project Team Builder Simulator   25

Chapter 3   Stakeholder Requirements and Value   51

Chapter 4   Scheduling   63

Chapter 5   Resource Management   83

Chapter 6   Budgeting   101

Chapter 7   Risk Management   117

Chapter 8   Project Integration — Planning, Executing
             Monitoring, and Controlling the Project   127

Chapter 9   Integration of Simulation-Based Training in Project
             Management Courses   141

Appendix   The Next Step — Creating and Managing Multiple
            Scenarios   157

Preface

In the global and technological 21st century, projects and project management have increased in importance and complexity. The competitiveness of the marketplace has driven businesses to accelerate the process of introducing new products and services. These new offerings are increasingly more technologically advanced. In order for a business to innovate and develop a new product or service, it must form and manage a cross-disciplinary project team, involving various functional areas, to implement the innovation. As the race to be the first entrant in a particular market has grown more competitive with higher payoff stakes (and higher penalties for losing the race), the project management function has gained in importance.

The process of educating and training project managers presents a dilemma to academicians. The project management discipline is, almost by definition, an applied discipline. A project manager grows by working on projects and confronting and dealing with unstructured and unplanned situations. In preparing a project management textbook, it is impossible to foresee all of the possible unknowns and uncertainties that may be encountered on a particular project. For example, the second author of this book received a call from a former student in August 2001. The student was working for a US domestic airline and was working on a project that was considering reducing the level of security required in airline terminals. The student was scheduled to fly to a US airport on September 11, 2001 in order to begin a beta-test of a reduced security protocol. Needless to say, this project did not get off the ground.

Project management is not a theoretical discipline with a heavy body of conceptual material like mathematics or physics. There are a few core methodologies, such as the Critical Path Method that form the basis of project management. In addition, many techniques from operations research, such as linear programming and simulation may be applied to problems that arise in project management. The question of preparation of a suitable project management curriculum for training university students is somewhat open. In our view, project management cannot be taught with a "cookbook" approach, as it is a discipline that seeks to manage uncertainty.

From our experience in teaching project management at universities around the world, we believe that experiential instruction is an optimal approach for training students. Naturally, students should be trained in the core project management methodologies. In addition, they require hands-on experience to supplement the material on methodology. They must try out and experiment, for themselves, using realistic project scenarios, the various project management methodologies. Students must experience for themselves the various trade-offs that a project manager must deliberate between involving cost, schedule, and scope of a project.

The first author of this book, in conjunction with the Technion in Haifa, Israel, developed a simulation-based software tool — Project Team Builder (PTB) — that enables students to plan and simulate the execution of realistic projects. A student version of the PTB software accompanies this book. We believe that simulation-based training is particularly appropriate for teaching project management. A project is a one-time endeavor that is intended to implement a new product or service. By its nature, a project seeks to implement an innovative technology or systems approach. A project manager and a project management team cannot solely rely on historical experience with past projects as a guide for managing a current project. A simulation-based tool allows a project manager to experience a dry run with a project plan, with little real-world impact should a mistake occur. Likewise, by using a simulation-based tool in their training, students can experience the types of decisions that may confront a project manager in practice. Students can propose various workarounds and suggestions for dealing with unplanned activities, and the simulation-based tool, in this case, the PTB, can provide immediate feedback on the quality of those decisions.

This book is intended to fill an unmet need in the project management textbook market. Each of the key project management functions is described — scheduling, budgeting, resource management, risk management, and quality control. Following the description of methodologies associated with a particular project management area, the book illustrates — using screen shots from the PTB tool — how these methodologies may be implemented on a realistic project. Thus, the book integrates project management methodology and PTB implementation throughout. By using the student version of the PTB software while reading through the text, a student reader may absorb project management methodologies both from study, as well as from hands-on experience. Chapter 9 discusses experiences from project management courses given throughout the world that integrated the PTB tool with standard project management methodologies.

Project management is an empirical discipline. In order to train new project managers, experiential learning is required. We believe that this book is unique in the project management field in its integration of project management concepts with a hands-on software tool that enables students to experiment and "touch" realistic project scenarios.

This book has been a collaborative effort. In particular, we wish to acknowledge and thank the contributions of the following Professors who contributed their personal experience, detailed in Chapter 9, of teaching project management with a simulation-based teaching approach and deployment of the PTB tool in their lectures and class exercises.

- Dr. Luis A. Chepote — Post-Graduate School at Universidad San Ignacio de Loyola (EPG USIL), Lima, Peru
- Dr. Angelika Kokkinaki — University of Nicosia, Nicosia Cyprus
- Dr. Rainer Kolisch — Technical University of Munich, School of Management, Munich, Germany
- Dr. Hariharan Subramanyan — L &T Institute of Project Management, Mumbai, India
- Mr. Matthew O'Rourke — Yale School of Management, New Haven, CT, USA

We are also grateful to Ms. Lillian Bluestein for her tireless efforts in proofreading and improving the writing style of the manuscript. Finally, we thank the many students that we taught and, hopefully, influenced, over the many years in teaching project management at our respective universities. Their questions and suggestions enhanced our methods for teaching project management.

Avraham Shtub
Moshe Rosenwein

About the Authors

Professor Avraham Shtub holds the Stephen and Sharon Seiden Chair in Project Management. He has a B.Sc. in Electrical Engineering from the Technion — Israel Institute of Technology (1974), an MBA from Tel Aviv University (1978) and a Ph.D. in Management Science and Industrial Engineering from the University of Washington (1982).

He is a certified Project Management Professional (PMP) and a member of the Project Management Institute (PMI-USA). He is the recipient of the Institute of Industrial Engineering 1995 "Book of the Year Award" for his book *Project Management: Engineering, Technology and Implementation* (co-authored with Jonathan Bard and Shlomo Globerson), Prentice Hall, 1994. He is the recipient of the Production Operations Management Society; Wick Skinner Teaching Innovation Achievements Award for his book *Enterprise Resource Planning (ERP): The Dynamics of Operations Management*. His books on Project Management have been published in English, Hebrew, Greek and Chinese.

He is the recipient of the 2008 Project Management Institute Professional Development Product of the Year Award for the training simulator "Project Team Builder — PTB". He is also the recipient of the IISE/Joint Publishers Book-of-the-Year Award 2017 for his book *Introduction to Industrial Engineering* (co-authored with Yuval Cohen).

Prof. Shtub was a Department Editor for *IIE Transactions* and was on the Editorial Boards of the *Project Management Journal*, *The International Journal of Project Management*, *IIE Transactions* and the *International*

Journal of Production Research. He was a faculty member of the Department of Industrial Engineering at Tel Aviv University from 1984 to 1998 where he also served as a chairman of the department (1993–1996). He joined the Technion in 1998 and was the Associate Dean and head of the MBA program.

He has been a consultant to industry in the areas of project management, training by simulators and the design of production — operation systems. He was invited to speak at special seminars on Project Management and Operations in Europe, the Far East, North America, South America and Australia.

Professor Shtub visited and taught at Vanderbilt University, The University of Pennsylvania, Korean Institute of Technology, Bilkent University in Turkey, Otego University in New Zealand, Yale University, Universidad Politécnica de Valencia, University of Bergamo in Italy.

Dr. Moshe Rosenwein has a B.S.E from Princeton University and a Ph.D. in Decision Sciences from the University of Pennsylvania. He has worked in industry throughout his professional career, applying management science modeling and methodologies to business problems in supply chain optimization, network design, customer relationship management, and scheduling.

He has served as an adjunct professor at Columbia University on multiple occasions over the past 20 years and developed a project management course for the School of Engineering that has been taught since 2009. He has also taught at Seton Hall University and Rutgers University.

Dr. Rosenwein has published over 20 refereed papers and has delivered numerous talks at universities and conferences. In 2001, he led an industry team that was a semi-finalist in the Franz Edelman competition for the practice of management science.

Chapter 1

Introduction to Project Management

1.1. Terms, Concepts and Difficulties of Project Management

The term *project* is defined by the Cambridge Dictionary Online as a piece of planned work or an activity that is finished over a period of time and intended to achieve a particular purpose. This broad definition suggests that everyone is involved in projects, and project management is important for anyone performing "planned work". The Project Management Institute publishes the Project Management Body of Knowledge (PMBOK) which, in its fifth edition, defines a project as a "temporary endeavor undertaken to create a unique product, service, or result."

The temporary, non-repetitive nature of projects suggests that anyone who manages a project faces several problems including the following:

(1) Since projects are unique, project managers and project teams are not repeating the same projects; they are not "riding the learning curve", i.e., improvement by mere repetition is limited. Structured learning and training activities are needed to enable project managers and their teams to practice, repeatedly, the tools and techniques they may use to manage a project. It is important to keep the cost of learning low and, more importantly, to minimize the cost and likelihood of making mistakes on real projects. One way to support learning and

1

to get ready for a new project is by simulating previous, current, and future projects in a lab-like environment.

(2) As a result of the non-repetitive nature of projects, project managers and project teams have little opportunity to collect data from identical, historical projects and to use it to support future decision making. This lack of data or "knowledge gap" is the source of risk in projects and the cause of many project failures. There is a need for "dry runs" or simulation of project activities and project plans prior to their actual implementation along with a well-structured process of data collection and analysis to improve project plans.

(3) Project teams are assembled for specific projects and, frequently, team members do not have prior experience of working together as a team. Team members need shared understanding of how project success is defined and measured, what needs to be done to achieve project success, how it should be done, when, and by whom. There is a need for team training and team building to create shared understanding of project goals and the best way to achieve those goals. A simulated environment where the team of a new project can "manage" the project together and develop shared understanding is one possible solution to this problem.

Our goal, in writing this book and using the student version of the simulation software, the Project Team Builder, that accompanies it, is to help anyone involved in projects deal with the above three problems. Specifically, this book is written for project managers and project teams, as well as graduate and undergraduate students, who want to learn and practice the basic tools of project management. This book presents tools and techniques commonly used to manage projects. It also describes and provides a simulation platform with which it is possible to simulate a large variety of projects in a safe, user-friendly environment.

Project management is defined by the Project Management Body of Knowledge (PMBOK) fifth edition as "the application of knowledge, skills, tools and techniques to project activities to meet the project requirements."

To achieve its goals, this book focuses on two issues:

1. It describes the simplest and commonly used knowledge, skills, tools, and techniques that project managers and their teams are using to manage projects; and
2. It facilitates hands-on training of individuals and teams by applying the knowledge, skills, tools, and techniques in a simulated environment.

The Project Team Builder, the software that comes with the book, provides a simulation environment in which project managers and their teams can practice these tools and techniques in a safe and inexpensive environment.

There are nine chapters in this book:

1. Introduction to Project Management
In this chapter, we present some of the terminology commonly used in project management. We also discuss the history of project management, focusing on the last one hundred years, as most of the tools and techniques presented in this book were developed during this period. The selection and initiation of projects is discussed and illustrated.
2. Introduction to the Project Team Builder (PTB) Simulator
In this chapter, we present the Project Team Builder simulator, its logic, and the major functions it supports. The PTB is based on the following principles:

   I. *A simulation approach*: The PTB simulates real or imaginary projects. Any project can be simulated by creating a scenario based on that project data and simulating the scenario using the PTB simulator.
  II. *A case study approach*: In the PTB, the information on the simulated project is presented in two ways — as scenario data and as a case study file that introduces the user to the "story" of the simulated project.
 III. *A dynamic approach*: Unlike traditional case studies that present a snapshot of reality as a specific situation at a given point of time, the user of PTB can control the simulation time and "execute" the project to see the dynamic behavior of the project and the interaction over time between project scope, schedule, and cost.

IV. *A model-based approach*: Simple tools and techniques commonly used for project management are built into the PTB including tools for scheduling, value analysis, budgeting, resource management, and risk management.

V. *A data-based approach*: All the data required to prepare a project plan and to execute it is available as part of the case study or scenario. The user does not have to input any data and can concentrate on analysis and decision making.

These principles are discussed in detail later in this book along with examples and screenshots to introduce the PTB to the reader.

3. Stakeholder Requirements and Value
Project success is measured by its ability to satisfy the needs and expectations of the stakeholders. In this chapter, we present the concepts of stakeholders and their needs and expectations. We discuss the terms *benefit* and *value* and ways to measure both. We show how the tools related to benefit and value are implemented in the PTB.

4. Scheduling
Project scheduling tools are probably the most commonly used tools. The need to estimate the duration of a project, to acquire long lead-time items, and scarce resources motivated the development of scheduling tools during the 20th century. Such tools, like the Gantt chart, are widely used today because they are simple to construct and to understand and, yet, provide essential information to the project manager, the project team, and other stakeholders. We present the concepts of the critical path and slack; we show how they are implemented in the PTB and how they are presented to the user. The impact of uncertainty on scheduling and the resulting risk are discussed and illustrated by the Monte Carlo simulation built into the PTB.

5. Resource Management
Resources are needed to perform project activities. Human resources, machines, equipment, and materials are frequently limited in their availability, and therefore the project plan must account for resource constraints. Furthermore, the efficient and effective use of resources is an important consideration in project planning. Tools like the resource graph or histogram are discussed, and their usage for project

planning is illustrated by the PTB. By integrating resource management with scheduling considerations, feasible schedules (with respect to resource availability) are developed. The availability of many types of resources is subject to uncertainty: machine breakdown, absenteeism of workers, and loss of material are examples of sources of risk that impact project success. Such uncertainties are introduced in the PTB, and the user can learn how to factor uncertainty into project planning processes.

6. Budgeting

   The project budget represents financial sources and the use of funds throughout the project life cycle. The budget is an important part of the plan, and it is based on estimates of income and cost. The direct cost of resources, as well as other costs, such as the cost of idle time or the penalty due to missed due dates, are presented in the project budget. The PTB shows historical (past) costs along with future (estimated) costs, as well as the cash flow and cash position of the project at any time.

7. Risk Management

   The non-repetitive nature of projects limits the amount of past information available to the project manager and the project management team as a basis for planning. A risk is an event with some probability and some expected outcomes that may occur during the course of a project and have an adverse effect on the project. A project manager must assess which risks are most likely to impact the ability of the project team to achieve the project goals and to satisfy its constraints. Risk management is an important consideration in project management. This activity should start very early in a project life cycle in an effort to identify risks and to analyze them as a basis for risk-related decisions. The initial analysis is performed as part of project initiation, as the level of risk associated with a proposed project is an important factor in the go/no go decision, i.e., a decision to start the project. Furthermore if the decision is "go", there might be different technological and operational alternatives to perform the project. The risk associated with each of these alternatives is a major factor in the decision as to which alternative to select for implementation. During the project planning phase, the decision whether to mitigate the risks (by eliminating, reducing, or transferring all or part of the risks identified) is crucial. Risk mitigation is an effort to reduce the risk or eliminate it altogether before the risk event takes place. Risks that are not mitigated, as well as residual risks left over after mitigation, may need a contingency plan or some sort of buffer or reserve as a protection. Such risks are monitored during project execution. Corrective actions are taken whenever a risk event takes place and derails a project from its original plan.

8. Project Integration — Planning, Executing, Monitoring, and Controlling the Project.

   Project plans represent the way management would like the project to be executed. Since these plans are based on limited information and there are risks that might derail the project from its planned course, a monitoring and control system is implemented. This system monitors the actual progress of the project and compares it to the plans. When actual progress deviates from project plans, root cause analysis is performed, and possible corrective actions are evaluated. A corrective action is taken when management decides that such an action is needed to bring the project back to the original plan.

   The different aspects of project management discussed so far are not independent. In other words, project scope management, project scheduling, cost management, resource management, and risk management are dependent on each other, and a decision may impact all or several of the above aspects.

   The project manager and the project team must understand the complex relationship between the different dimensions of the project. The PTB simulator is designed to demonstrate these complex relationships and to help the user understand how a potential decision may impact the project — for example, how a decision to add resources might impact cost or quality. By executing, monitoring, and controlling different scenarios, the user engages in the art and science of project management while minimizing the cost of making poor decisions.

9. A Review of how Simulation-Based Training is Integrated in Project Management Courses.

   In this chapter, we present short reports of users of the PTB simulator. Simulation-Based Training (SBT) can be integrated with lectures, books, and traditional case studies. We hope that the experience of several users will help the reader decide how SBT can fit into a specific setting.

1.2. Project Life Cycle and Major Components of Project Management

Project management has been widely practiced throughout history, dating back to the construction of the Egyptian pyramids almost 5000 years ago. As a discipline, project management is becoming increasingly important for business and government. For example, as product life cycles continue to decrease, new products and services are introduced with increased pressure on firms to rapidly go to market. Even if a firm cannot be the first entrant in a particular market, it can achieve greater profits by being as fast as possible in entering into an existing market. McKinsey estimated that a firm loses 12% of its profitability from a product over its life cycle if the product is three months delayed in getting to market. The penalty for being late to market increases to 25% reduced profitability if a delay is five months.

Project management is a very empirical discipline. Hands-on work experience is necessary for an individual to develop into a capable and successful project manager. The key methodologies in the field were developed in industry — not in academia. In the 1910s, the Gantt chart scheduling method was developed by Henry Gantt. In the 1950s, the Critical Path Method (CPM) was developed at DuPont. At roughly the same time, the consulting firm, Booz, Allen, and Hamilton, working on behalf of the US Navy's Special Project Office, developed the Program Evaluation and Review Technique (PERT) to support the Polaris missile project. Since then, numerous tools and techniques were developed to support project management. This effort is still on-going; practitioners and researchers in academia are working on new tools and techniques, as well as on the improvement of existing ones.

The project management function was often handled in an ad hoc fashion by many organizations. A manager, from a line organization that was relevant to a particular project, would be selected to manage and run the project. Today, project management is a recognized discipline, and firms are hiring managers, trained and experienced in project management, to lead projects. Projects have become increasingly complex, spanning multiple disciplines in a business. A project manager must build and sustain cross-functional teams in order for a project to be successful. The increasing technological and organizational complexity of a project has required businesses to establish a project management office in order to support and carry out a large-scale project work stream.

A project, unlike a process, is a one-time, temporary endeavor undertaken to create a new or unique product or service. Unlike process management, which seeks to eliminate variability and create a repeatable set of tasks, project management accepts variability due to the uniqueness of the endeavor. A project manager's job would be quite straightforward if a project plan ran smoothly without any bumps along the way. In practice, a project invariably deviates from plan. For example, project scope is modified by key stakeholders due to changing business conditions. A project may experience a schedule delay or a cost overrun due to changing economic conditions, unforeseen quality issues, or uncertain technologies not performing as expected. Project management is also concerned with resource management, including personnel. The possibility of conflict arising within a team is another source of uncertainty. A project manager's responsibility is to mitigate risks early on and to plan for and execute contingency plans to manage and cope with uncertainty.

The content of a project is divided into stages (or phases), and the collection of such stages is known as the project life cycle. A simple life cycle form may have four phases performed in sequence (a phase starts only after its predecessor phase is finished).

I. Formulation and selection
II. Planning
III. Scheduling and control
IV. Implementation and termination

In the formulation and selection phase, key stakeholders' needs and expectations are translated into a business need — to formulate project ideas addressing that need. In this phase, a high-level project scope is sketched out. If the proposed project is selected for further development, alternative technological and operational ways to perform the project are proposed and evaluated. Proposals will typically be evaluated based on their ability to satisfy stakeholders' needs and expectations, as well as technological and economic feasibility, the level of risk involved, and cost and schedule considerations. When an alternative is selected, a more detailed project plan is created in the planning phase. Specific high-level tasks are identified, including an estimate of resources and costs that will be needed. The heart of a project plan is the scheduling and control phase when resources are assigned to each project task, and the project idea, formulated in earlier phases, is realized. Finally, a project concludes with implementation that ends when a product or service is handed off to a user environment. For example, a product prototype developed by the project team would be moved to a factory production environment in this final phase.

This simple project life cycle approach that was common for many years is a sequential approach. In the software development industry, it is known as the "Waterfall" life cycle. In the Waterfall life cycle, project phases are performed in sequence with no overlapping. In some cases, a "gate" is introduced between consecutive phases and, only after passing this gate successfully, does the project proceed to the next phase. For example, a Preliminary Design Review (PDR) may be the gate that separates the formulation and selection phase and the planning phase, and a Critical Design Review (CDR) may be the gate that separates the planning phase and the execution phase.

Another life cycle approach is the "Spiral" approach in which the project scope is divided into several smaller projects. The first one aims at delivering the Minimum Viable Product (MVP) — a product configuration with the minimum features and functions that will provide enough value to justify acceptance by the stakeholders. In consecutive iterations of the spiral, more features and functions are added to the product based on the feedback from users and adopters. The advantage of this approach is a short time to market. A third life cycle approach is the "Incremental or Agile" project in which short development cycles are used to incrementally add more and more functions and features to the point that the product becomes MVP.

Although each project has a unique set of goals, there is enough commonality at a generic level to permit the development of a unified framework for planning and control. Project management techniques are designed to handle the common processes and problems that arise during a project's life cycle.

The following list contains some of the major components of a "typical" project.

(1) Project initiation, selection, and definition
   1.1 Identification of needs
   1.2 Identification of stakeholders
   1.3 Development of alternatives
   1.4 Evaluation of alternatives based on performance (quality), cost, duration, and risk
   1.5 Selection of the "most promising" alternative and gaining approval

(2) Project organization
   2.1 Development of a project governance structure, including identification of functional areas that will participate in the project
   2.2 Structuring the project's work content into increasingly smaller work modules using a work breakdown structure (WBS)
   2.3 Allocation of WBS elements to participating organizations and assigning managers to the lowest level of the WBS hierarchy, known as work packages
   2.4 Development of communication and reporting protocols

(3) Analysis of activities
   3.1 Definition of the project's major activities
   3.2 Development of a list of subactivities required to complete each activity
   3.3 Development of precedence relations among activities
   3.4 Development of project flow, typically modeled with a network diagram
   3.5 Establishment of milestones

(4) Project scheduling
   4.1 Development of a calendar to track the progress of a project's activities

4.2 Assignment of resources to activities and estimation of activity durations

4.3 Monitoring progress and milestones and updating the schedule

(5) Resource management
    5.1 Estimation of resource requirements for each activity
    5.2 Acquisition of resources
    5.3 Allocation of resources among a project's activities
    5.4 Monitoring resource usage and cost

(6) Risk management
    6.1 Identification of risks (technological, personnel, etc.)
    6.2 Proactive risk management and mitigation
    6.3 Reactive risk management and control

(7) Project budgeting
    7.1 Forecast of direct and indirect costs
    7.2 Estimation of cash flow for each period over a project's expected life cycle
    7.3 Development of an overall project budget
    7.4 Monitoring actual cost

(8) Project execution and control
    8.1 Development and execution of data collection and data analysis systems
    8.2 Execution of activities
    8.3 Identification of deviations in cost, scope, schedule, and quality
    8.4 Development and implementation of corrective plans

(9) Project termination and evaluation
    9.1 Evaluation of project success
    9.2 Recommendations for improvement in project management practices

1. *Project initiation, selection, and definition.* A project idea starts with identifying a need for a new service, product, process, or system. It may be initiated by one or more internal stakeholders or it may be initiated by an external source. If the underlying need is considered significant, a study of alternative solution approaches is, then, initiated. Each proposed alternative is evaluated based upon an agreed set of performance measures. The most promising alternatives, based on performance, duration, costs, and risks, comprise an "efficient frontier" of possible solutions.

Due to inherent uncertainty of executing a project (a unique, one-time, business endeavor), most financial and technological estimates are likely to be problematic. For each activity, a project manager must assess the risks associated with completing the activity as per the project plan. A risk assessment includes estimating a probability of an unplanned event occurring and an estimate of the unplanned event's impact on the overall project plan. A proactive risk management approach identifies major risk drivers at a project's inception. Some of these risks may be avoided or mitigated by changing plans or reduced to an acceptable level. Remaining risks (or residual risks) are monitored throughout the project execution. Sometimes, contingency plans should be prepared to handle unfavorable events if and when they occur.

Once an alternative is chosen, design details are specified during the project's concept formulation and definition phase. Preliminary design efforts culminate with a configuration baseline. The features and functions of the selected alternative should satisfy stakeholders' needs and expectations in order to be accepted and approved by management. A well-structured and transparent project proposal selection and evaluation process, involving all interested parties, increases the likelihood of management approval and project success.

2. *Project organization.* Many stakeholders participate in a particular project. In a project's advanced development phase, a Statement of Work (SOW) is drafted to define the work content. A set of project activities are defined and arranged hierarchically in a tree-like format, known as a Work Breakdown Structure (WBS). The relationship between functional organizations participating in a project, known as the Organizational Breakdown Structure (OBS), is similarly depicted.

In an OBS, the lines of communication between and within organizations participating in a project are defined. Similarly, procedures and templates for work authorization and reporting are established. Lowest-level WBS elements form work packages. A manager in the OBS is assigned responsibility for each work package.

At the conclusion of a project's advanced development phase, a detailed budget and cash flow are prepared and submitted for management approval.

3. *Analysis of activities*. In order to identify required resources and to prepare a detailed schedule, a project management team must develop a detailed list of required activities. These activities are proposed to accomplish the WBS tasks in an efficient and effective manner. Each work stream in the initial planning phase typically consists of many activities. A feasible project plan requires that precedence relations be introduced to link a project's activities. Precedence relations, that model various technological and logistical constraints inherent in a project, are typically represented graphically in the form of a network model by project management software packages.

Completion of a significant project activity defines a milestone. Milestones provide feedback to stakeholders and senior-level management and signal progress on the project. They form the basis for budgeting, scheduling, and resource management. As a project ensues, the project plan and associated project schedule are updated to account for modified and new activities in the WBS, the successful completion of activities, and any changes in design, organization, and requirements due to uncertainty or changes in market conditions.

4. *Project scheduling*. The expected durations of activities are important for both financial and operational planning. Funds must be set aside in a timely fashion and resources must be procured in a timely fashion in order for a project to realize its milestones. Project scheduling starts with a calendar, specifying available working hours per day, available working days per week, holidays, etc. The project management team estimates the expected duration of each activity. A project schedule is then developed based on the calendar, precedence constraints among activities, and each activity's expected duration time. A project schedule specifies the starting and ending dates of each activity and any slack or leeway. A project schedule is an input into the budgeting and resource management processes. It is also used as a basis for work authorization and as a baseline for monitoring a project's progress. The schedule is updated throughout a project's life cycle so that project monitoring and control is up to date.

5. *Resource management.* Activities are performed by resources based on project requirements. These requirements form the basis of resource management and resource acquisition planning.

If resource requirements exceed expected availability, schedule delays may occur. A project manager must take action in these cases either by acquiring additional resources or by subcontracting. Alternatively, a project manager may reschedule activities (especially those with slack) in order to "smooth" demand for resources and not exceed expected resource availability. Other potential tactics for dealing with gaps between resource supply and demand, such as maximizing resource utilization, may be available as well.

During a project's execution phase, resources are allocated periodically to activities according to a predetermined timetable. Since actual and planned resource usage often differ, a project manager must monitor progress against the project plan. Low utilization and higher-than-planned costs or resource consumption rates should promptly be reported to senior-level management. Large discrepancies between planned and actual resource output may require significant alterations in a project's schedule.

6. *Risk management.* Risk management starts with an effort to identify risk — unplanned events that may occur and, if they do, the project may not achieve its goals or may violate some of its constraints. Typical sources of risk are technological, financial, political, and resource related. Identified risks are analyzed by qualitative and quantitative tools, High-risk events should be mitigated *a priori* — as part of project planning. When new technologies are developed or deployed, risks associated with technological alternatives must be evaluated. In addition, quality tests to validate operational and technical requirements must be designed, and contingency plans should be prepared. Changes in requirements or in market conditions may necessitate modifications to the configuration. Technology experts should be part of the project team in order to ensure that a project achieves its approved configuration. These subject-matter technology experts can evaluate proposed changes, introduce approved changes into the configuration plan, and develop a quality management program. The quality management program seeks to prevent defects and to continuously improve processes. Ultimately, the quality management program increases the likelihood that a project's deliverables will meet project specifications as stipulated by stakeholders and senior management.

Throughout project execution, a risk management plan is updated as new information is made available. Risks are monitored, as early detection of a risk event can trigger corrective actions to bring a project back to its planned course.

7. *Project budgeting*. Preparation of a budget results in a time-phased plan that summarizes expected costs, revenue, cash flow, and milestones. A budget is derived by estimating the cost of activities and resources. As a project schedule tracks activities and resources over time, it serves a basis for a cash flow analysis. If the cash flow and/or the resulting budget are not acceptable to a project's funding source, for example, senior management, then the project schedule must be modified. For example, a project manager may delay activities that have slack, as delaying these activities will minimize the impact on the overall project duration.

Once a budget is approved, it serves as a baseline financial tool for the project. A project manager can proceed to establish credit lines and loans, and the cost of financing the project can be evaluated. As a project progresses, information on actual cost is gathered and compared with the original project budget. By comparing actual and planned costs, a project management team can effectively oversee the financial aspect of a project.

8. *Project execution and control*. A feasible schedule integrates milestone deadlines, budget constraints, resource availability, and technological requirements, while satisfying resource constraints and the precedence relations among activities.

An initial project schedule inevitably is subject to unexpected or random events that are difficult (or impossible) to predict. Project control systems are designed with three objectives: (1) to identify deviations and to forecast future deviations between actual project plans and work actually completed; (2) to identify the root causes of these deviations; and (3) to support management decisions aimed at righting the course of the project.

Project control requires timely collection and analysis of project performance data. A project management team should continually monitor costs, resource usage, and achievement of milestones. Actual and planned performance in each of these areas should be compared. Deviations in any area (e.g., schedule delay) may trigger deviations in other areas (e.g., cost overrun).

All project operational data collected by a project control system are analyzed. If deviations are detected by the project management team, then corrective actions might be devised to correct a project's course. The existing project plan is modified accordingly.

During a project's life cycle, a project manager is continuously updating original estimates of completion dates and costs. Updated estimates are used by the management to evaluate a project's progress and the efficiency of participating organizations. Management evaluations form the basis of forecasts concerning expected project success at each stage of its life cycle.

9. *Project termination.* A project does not terminate when its technical objectives are met. Management should derive lessons learned from a completed project in order to improve management of future projects. A project management team should conduct a detailed analysis of the original plan, modifications made over the course of a project, the actual progress, and the success of the project. A project "postmortem" seeks to identify processes and techniques that were not effective and to recommend improvements. As part of the evaluation, a project management team should identify missing or redundant managerial tools. New techniques should be adopted when appropriate, and obsolete procedures and tools may be discarded.

Information on the cost and duration of activities, once completed, and the cost and utilization of resources, once deployed, should be stored to support planning of future projects.

1.3. Project Success

The success of a project is measured by the stakeholders, typically across at least three dimensions known as the project triangle: cost, schedule, and quality/scope. The first two criteria — cost and schedule — are quantitative metrics that can be explicitly tracked. However, a project can suffer from cost overruns and schedule delays and, nevertheless, be deemed a success. For example, the movie *Titanic* was released several years after its initial forecast release date with a budget overrun of close to 100%. Yet, it won numerous industry awards and was the first movie to gross over $1 billion in revenue.

In addition to cost and schedule, a project is evaluated by the value that it brings to its stakeholders. Specifically, did a project meet or exceed the goals that were laid out in the original project plan that was approved by stakeholders? Often, a project's goals are revised in mid-stream due to changing internal and market factors. In this case, a project's ultimate deliverables can be measured with respect to originally stated goals, accounting for the changes that were requested and accounting for the technical and business issues that were encountered in order to incorporate requested and needed changes. In some instances, a project can be compared to other projects in the organization with respect to delivering on project milestones. In practice, an organization may arrive at an overall perception of a project based on various internal and political considerations.

In general, a project seeks to achieve goals in three dimensions: cost, schedule, and quality/scope (the project triangle). Typically, a project manager must make a trade-off between these three dimensions — for example, delivering a project on schedule by going over budget and hiring additional resources or working overtime. The dimensions of critical importance will vary with the type of project. For example, a project to develop the halftime entertainment at the Super Bowl must be completed by the time of the Super Bowl, regardless of cost overruns. There is no credit given if the show is ready one day late, but under budget. Likewise, a project to develop a new automobile feature must emphasize scope or quality of the deliverable. In this case, delivery of a faulty product — but delivering on time and within budget — is meaningless, as customer safety is paramount.

Project performance has improved over time, although significant room for improvement exists. The Chaos Report, which tracks Information Technology (IT) project performance, reported that, in 1995, 16% of IT projects surveyed were completed on time and within budget. By 2011, 37% of IT projects were completed on time and within budget. Conversely, in 1995, 30% of surveyed IT projects were cancelled prior to completion. This figure declined to 21% by 2011. Performance issues were particularly prevalent in large projects (projects with labor content > $10MM). Only 10% of large projects were considered successful, whereas 38% failed entirely. In contrast, 76% of small projects (projects with labor content < $1MM) were successful, and only 4% failed. This high level of success among small projects justifies, in part, the spiral and the agile project development.

In a 2006 study, the Standish Group investigated root causes for project failure. In surveying organizations, the study found that overoptimistic estimates concerning risk factors and the ability to develop new technologies and processes coupled with project scope changes were the leading root causes of project failure. The learning from this study is that project managers should realistically set expectations for stakeholders at the outset of a project. Although a project manager should, in general, be optimistic and passionate, they should also be candid and broad-minded in assessing risks and potential pitfalls.

The success of a project can also be tied to various factors. Among the most prominent root causes of a project's success are: (i) clearly defined project goals and objectives whereby each individual on the project understands his/her role and how that role contributes to the overall project; (ii) top management support, which leads to support of resources and personnel that are needed to successfully execute a project; and (iii) effective communication channels whereby a project manager or the project management office is communicating on a consistent basis with a consistent message to all project stakeholders and participants.

1.4. Project Initiation, Selection, and Definition

Although this book focuses on methods and tools to support project planning and execution, project selection (which is part of portfolio management) is an equally important business process. In selecting a project or a portfolio of projects to undertake, a business needs to consider the risk/reward trade-off. In general, a business seeks projects that maximize net present value while not exceeding some risk threshold. In addition, resource constraints involving both funding and personnel availability may influence the decision of whether to undertake a project at a particular point in time. For example, an organization may highly value a proposed project, but may defer its execution until additional funding may be available from its parent company. In a constrained business environment, rather than making a go/no go decision regarding a project (i.e., embarking on a project proposal in its entirety or rejecting it outright), a firm may elect to modify a project's scope or duration and fund a portion of the originally proposed project.

Various factors influence an organization's decision on whether to undertake a project.

1. *Strategic factors* — An organization may feel a competitive necessity to embark on a project. An organization may desire to keep a foothold in a particular market so as to not fall behind its competition. A project may also represent a market expansion opportunity. For example, quite a few early e-commerce projects were financial losers for many years. However, businesses had the foresight to envision a "digital" world in which virtual shopping would increase in popularity and profitability. Some projects are undertaken because the ultimate deliverable product or service is consistent with an organization's mission. For example, the popular automobile manufacturers will regularly update their family sedan line, since this product is a staple in this industry. Finally, a project may be undertaken, as it may be perceived to enhance a company's image; for example, sponsorship of a major sporting event.
2. *Portfolio factors* — An organization typically seeks to diversify the set of projects that it undertakes at any given time. For example, an automobile manufacturer will produce a full line of cars and trucks — not only high-end models that are most profitable. A pharmaceutical manufacturer may undertake development of a range of medicines across various disease states. Some of its compounds may be of a "me too" variety, as they emulate existing medicines in the market with

respect to efficacy and safety. The research and development effort on "me too" compounds is typically less risky, and the probability of successful clinical trials is high. In contrast, some of a pharmaceutical manufacturer's research and development program may be devoted to discovering breakthroughs in disease areas with significant unmet needs. In these cases, the probability of developing a safe product with improved efficacy is low, but the commercial and societal benefit, if successful, is quite rewarding. In addition to balancing risk, an organization's project portfolio (sometimes referred to as a product pipeline) needs to balance cash flow and resource usage. For example, certain key developers may be required for a number of lucrative proposed projects. If only a finite number of such resources are available at any particular time and if significant barriers exist in acquiring similar resources, an organization may have to defer some profitable projects to a later date when required resources become available.

If a project proposal is accepted and funded by stakeholders, a project plan is developed by the project manager (or project management office) and shared with stakeholders. A project plan contains additional details of the project, beyond those specified in the proposal. A project plan will describe roles and responsibilities of each project subteam and the project governance committee. A plan outlines a tentative project schedule with key milestones and project checkpoints. A high-level budget, including placeholders for subcontractors, is provided. A plan may also specify processes for change management — stakeholders seeking to modify project requirements in mid-stream — and quality management — user approval of milestone deliverables.

A critical component of a project plan is a WBS. A WBS is a hierarchy that has the project's ultimate product or service deliverable at its apex. Successive levels of the WBS hierarchy provide increasingly detailed identification of individual tasks that constitute the production of the end product. The lowest level of a WBS hierarchy is known as Work Packages (WP). Associated with each WP are required resources, budget, duration time, performance measures, and a specific deliverable date.

The following example illustrates a WBS. Consider a project to develop an MBA curriculum in a university (Level 1). The second level of the WBS consists of developing courses in each of the major disciplines required in a business school; for example, marketing, finance, accounting, and management. The third level of the WBS involves planning and developing course content for a line of courses in a discipline. For example, the finance line would break out into courses such as "Introduction to Finance", "Corporate Finance", and "International Finance." The third level of the WBS, in this example, would correspond to WPs, as individual professors and instructors may be assigned to develop each course within a specified time period and with specified funding.

1.5. Project Management from Art to Science

Megaprojects like the pyramids in Egypt, the temple in Jerusalem, or the road systems and water systems of the Roman Empire were completed successfully thousands of years ago. There is little record of the tools and techniques used to manage those megaprojects. Is it possible that complex projects of the ancient world were managed without using tools and techniques? We do not know for sure, but we do know that, even today, project management is a combination of art and science: some parts of project management are hard to teach using traditional lectures, books, or exercises. On-the-job training and work experience are essential for development of project managers.

Consider some human aspects of project management. Projects are performed by humans (such as project managers and project teams) to generate value or benefits for humans (the stakeholders). The success of a project is judged by the ability of its deliverables to satisfy the needs and expectations of the stakeholders. These needs and expectations are not always fully known early on in the project life cycle and, therefore, continuous communication with stakeholders throughout a project life cycle is a key success factor. A project manager needs communication skills to communicate not only with stakeholders, but also with team members and other parties involved in the project, like suppliers, subcontractors, regulators, project team members, and the internal management team. Some communication skills can be taught and practiced; other skills are the gift of God (also known as charisma) and may be hard or impossible to teach. This is one of the reasons that project management is considered by many to be a combination of art and science.

Another gift of God that project managers need is an ability to motivate their team and to lead team members, sometimes with limited authority. This is the case whenever some (or all) of the team members are not working full time on the project and (or) are not fully committed to the project. As an example, consider a functional organization in which members of the organization are grouped into functional units, such as an engineering department or a marketing division. The project manager in such organizations may be a coordinator that coordinates the work of different functions. The project manager usually has full responsibility for the success of the project but has limited authority over the people performing project activities. In some organizations, a project manager must work through the functional managers to get things done.

Another example of a project organization structure is a matrix organization. In this case, a project manager has some authority, as the organizational structure is a combination of the functional structure and the project-oriented structure. However, the project manager in a matrix organization shares authority with functional managers and has to coordinate with them. In both the functional structure and the matrix structure, communication skills are very important as is the ability of the project manager to take full responsibility of the project with limited authority. Understanding the internal politics of the organization and how to "get things done" is another important but hard-to-teach skill.

Even in a project-oriented organizational structure, a project manager may not be able to select the project team members; a project team may be formed prior to the nomination of the project manager. Alternatively, team members may be selected based on which individuals are available at the time the project is initiated.

Development of shared understanding of project goals and constraints as well as shared understanding of the way the project team members should work together is a crucial step in team formation. In many projects, shared understanding is developed "on the job" during project planning or, even later, during project execution. The price is a low performing team and conflicts among team members during early, important phases of the project. Research found that teams that used simulation to analyze alternative project plans and performed dry runs of the execution of selected project plans developed shared understanding among team members much earlier (Shtub *et al.* 2014).

The use of simulators to support the development of shared understanding and team formation is still a relatively new idea. Early research findings suggest that this might introduce more "science" into project management and improve project success rates (Iluz *et al.* 2015).

1.6. Summary

Project management is the art and science of planning and executing a non-repetitive effort to achieve specific goals while satisfying the needs and expectations of project stakeholders. Due to the non-repetitive nature of projects, learning by repetition and the impact of the learning curve are rather limited. The non-repetitive nature of projects causes knowledge gaps, uncertainty, and risks that must be managed throughout the project life cycle. This book presents the tools and techniques that support project management. The Project Team Builder simulator that accompanies the book provides an opportunity for practicing these tools and techniques in a safe simulated environment.

References

Salas, E., Wildman, J. I. and Piccolo, R. F. (2009). Using simulation-based training (SBT) to enhance management education, *The Academy of Management Learning and Education*, **8**(4), pp. 559–573.

Shtub, A. (1999). *Enterprise Resource Planning (ERP): The Dynamics of Operations Management*, Kluwer Academic Publishers, Boston.

Shtub, A., Parush, A. and Hewett, T. (2009). Guest editorial: The use of simulation in learning and teaching, *International Journal of Engineering Education*, **25**(2), pp. 206–209.

Iluz, M., Moser, B. and Shtub, A. (2015). Shared awareness among project team members through role-based simulation during planning — a comparative study. *Procedia Computer Science*, **44**, pp. 295–304.

Shtub, A., Iluz, M., Gersing, K., Oehmen, J. and Dubinsky, Y. (2014). Implementation of lean engineering practices in projects and programs through simulation based training, *PM World Journal*, **3**(3) pp. 1–13.

Chapter 2

Introduction to the Project Team Builder Simulator

2.1. Simulation-Based Training in Project Management

Teaching project management is not an easy task. Part of the difficulty is the one-of-a-kind or non-repetitive nature of projects. In teaching project management, we must consider a very wide array of possible situations (scenarios) with which the project manager and the project management team must learn to cope.

Traditionally, project management is taught using lectures, textbooks, articles, and case studies. Textbooks present a body of knowledge in the project management area including models, tools, and techniques. Many textbooks integrate some case studies so that the reader has an opportunity to implement the tools and techniques presented in the text. These case studies are valuable and widely used, but they suffer from an inherent shortcoming — they are static in nature.

Albert Einstein said: "Learning is experience. Everything else is just information."

This idea is implemented by Simulation-Based Training (SBT). Simulators provide users with an opportunity to experience complex and realistic situations in a "hands-on" fashion. Users may propose alternative strategies for dealing with multidimensional and uncertain business and engineering situations, and the simulator can efficiently feedback outcomes for different scenarios.

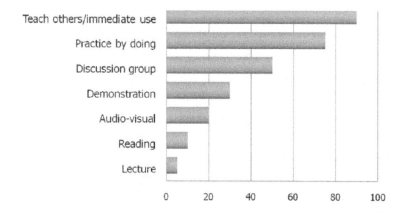

Fig. 2.1. Claimed effectiveness of different learning techniques (Kasser *et al.*, 2008)

Kasser *et al.* (2008) suggest that practice by doing is one of the most effective ways to learn, second only to teaching, as illustrated in Fig. 2.1.

The SBT is widely used in military training. Prior to the advent of computers, sandbox models and war games were used by military personnel to simulate different scenarios. An interesting example is the Chess game (Murray and Ruthven, 1913). Today, computer simulations are still used for military training.

The use of computer-based simulation for training in project management is relatively new. Examples include:

- Fissure SimProject
- Harvard Business School: Project Management Simulation
- SimulTrain
- Sharkworld

These simulators are designed to enhance the learning process by providing a safe environment in which a user can experience the use of project management tools and techniques without any downside for making the wrong decisions.

A common feature of these simulators is that all relevant information about a project is built into the simulator and is readily available to the user to plan and execute a project. These tools, however, are designed such that a specific project scenario is built into the simulator tool, and the scenario cannot be modified by a user; for example, to modify parameters such as the cost of resources or duration times of tasks. A user is, therefore, locked into a particular project instance and cannot experience planning projects in different industries.

The Project Team Builder (PTB) is designed to overcome this problem by separating the scenario building process from the simulator engine.

2.2. The Project Team Builder

The PTB is an SBT platform designed to simulate a large variety of projects. In the PTB, the scenario or case study is separated from the simulation engine. The simulator has a special editor called the Scenario Builder which is used to develop new project scenarios. The output of the Scenario Builder is a scenario file that a user can deploy to plan and execute a project. A large variety of scenarios was developed over the years by students and instructors.

Figure 2.2 displays the roles of the PTB Scenario Builder and the PTB Simulator in the learning process.

1. **The Scenario Builder** is used to create new scenarios or to modify existing ones. This process has three major steps:

   I. *Define problem space*: In building a new scenario, all relevant project data are collected with the help of a tree-like model contained in the Scenario Builder. Entities like activities or resources can be added at the appropriate level of the tree. When an entity is created, a checklist of attributes is displayed, and the user adds relevant data for each attribute.

   II. *Conceive solution options*: Each scenario can present several levels of alternatives:

   ➢ The first level is the project level. Several project workstreams may be linked together to form a solution to a given business or engineering problem. For example, a city looking for a solution to its public transportation problems may consider a light rail system, an underground (subway) system, or a bus system, as well as a combination of these alternatives. Each mass transit option is a different project workstream in the scenario.

➤ The second level is the activity level. Project activities may be performed by different teams of resources. For example, if a light rail system is considered, different suppliers of equipment may be necessary for purchasing activities and different contractors or subcontractors may be necessary for construction activities. This is known as the mode of execution of the activity.

➤ The third level is the detailed project plan including when to schedule each activity, the resources to assign to each activity, and tactics to acquire these resources.

All these alternatives may be built into a scenario so that a user can experiment with different combinations of alternatives in an effort to find the best plan possible.

III. *Identify ideal solution criteria*: This step is based on the needs and expectations of the stakeholders. Performance measures are defined for the requirements, for example, the range of a radar system. Specific performance goals are associated with each performance measure, such as the required project duration, its cost, the required range of the radar, etc. Based on the values of the specified performance measures, as determined by the simulation of a particular alternative, a user can select the best option.

2. **The PTB Simulator** is used to simulate the scenarios built by the Scenario Builder. This process has four major steps:

I. *Trade-off analysis is performed to find an optimal solution*: This step is performed using the tools and techniques discussed in this book and built into the PTB Simulator. Time, cost, and performance of alternative project plans are analyzed, and the best plans are selected for further analysis. This analysis introduces the impact of uncertainty and risk which is analyzed using the Monte Carlo simulator built into the PTB. Based on an analysis of various scenarios, the preferred option is selected for further evaluation.

II. *A detailed project plan is prepared* in this step using scheduling, budgeting, resource management, and risk management tools built into the PTB. The plan integrates all aspects of the project including the performance of the deliverables.

III. *The project plan is implemented by the simulation engine in a dynamic, stochastic environment.* The impact of uncertainty is analyzed, and the effects of different risk mitigation plans and project control on performance are fed back to the user. Based on the simulation results, a user can fine-tune the plan in an effort to improve it as much as possible. The solution is implemented by the Simulator period by period. A user can, thereby, monitor and control the simulation and take corrective actions, when necessary, at any period. At the end of each run, the PTB produces a detailed report, summarizing the results of executing the project plan that was selected.

IV. *The project report is analyzed in order to find the root cause of any deviations from the plan,* such as not achieving project goals or violating any project constraints. Improvements may be made to the plan, and a new, improved plan may be simulated again. The process of running a scenario, examining the output, and modifying inputs and assumptions terminates when a user is satisfied with a plan and the results of its implementation.

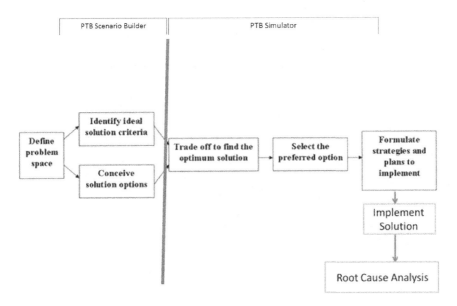

Fig. 2.2. The Scenario Builder and the PTB Simulator

In many projects, the goal is to satisfy performance and quality requirements while minimizing the cost of the project and its duration. In some projects, there are constraints on minimum acceptable performance and quality and on the maximum acceptable cost and duration of the project. Other goals and constraints may be added, for example, a constraint on the availability of some rare resources or precedence constraints on the order in which project activities can be executed. In the following chapters, we will discuss commonly-used tools and techniques designed to help a project manager and project team develop a good feasible project plan, i.e., a plan that does not violate any project constraints.

As an example, consider the radar development scenarios contained in the student version of the PTB. A performance goal is to maximize the range of the radar system. A related constraint is the minimum acceptable range for the radar system. Another goal is to finish the project as early as possible and not to exceed the required due date or the required duration of the project. In some scenarios, a penalty may apply in case of late completion while a bonus may be paid if the project is finished before its due date. There might be constraints on the availability of resources and the availability of funds as well.

The user has to develop a project plan that will achieve the goals and not violate any of the constraints, applying commonly-used project management tools and techniques that are discussed in the following chapters and are built into the PTB Simulator. Once a plan is developed, the user can execute the plan using the simulation engine. The user can monitor project progress and execute corrective actions whenever uncertainty causes actual progress to deviate from the project plan, triggering a risk of not satisfying project constraints or not achieving project goals.

2.3. The Radar Development Scenario

A radar system uses electromagnetic waves to determine the range and direction of objects such as aircraft. A radar antenna transmits pulses of energy generated by the transmitter. These pulses bounce off any object in their path. The energy returned to the receiving antenna (in some radar systems, the same antenna transmits and receives the pulses) is transferred to the receiver where it is analyzed to find the location (and, in some cases, the speed) of the object.

The main components of a radar system are: (1) the transmitter that emits electromagnetic waves in predetermined directions via the transmitting antenna, (2) the receiving antenna, and (3) the receiver. The transmitter power (the amount of energy transmitted), the antenna gain, and the sensitivity of the receiver impact the range of the radar system.

In the scenarios provided with the PTB student version, the project manager (i.e., the user) must oversee a new radar system development project.

The project consists of five tasks:

1. Systems engineering — deciding on the required specifications of the main components — the transmitter, the antenna, and the receiver — that will satisfy the required specifications for the overall radar system
2. Antenna design and manufacturing
3. Transmitter design and manufacturing
4. Receiver design and manufacturing
5. Integration of the different components into a complete radar system, and testing and commissioning of the system.

The project has a due date. Also, there is a penalty for late completion and a bonus for early completion.

Two types of resources are used in the project: Engineers and Technicians.

The availability of these resources is limited. A cost is associated with the use of these resources, including an idle cost that accrues when resources assigned to the project are not utilized.

A required range is specified for the radar system, say, 12 miles. Also, quality and reliability conditions are specified.

The radar range is determined by the radar equation:

$$\text{Range} = \sqrt[4]{[TP]*[RS]*[AG]},$$

where TP is the Transmitter Power, RS is the Receiver Sensitivity, and AG is the Antenna Gain.

The Quality is determined by the following equation:

$$Quality = [SEQ] * [QT] * [QR] * [QA] * [QI] * 100,$$

where SEQ is Quality of the Systems Engineering effort, QT is Quality of the Transmitter, QR is Quality of the Receiver, QA is Quality of the Antenna, and QI is Quality of the Integration effort.

The Reliability is determined by the following equation:

$$Reliability = [AR] * [IR] * [TR] * [RR] * 100,$$

where AR is Reliability of the Antenna, IR is Reliability of the Integration effort, TR is Reliability of the Transmitter, and RR is Reliability of the Receiver.

The task of the project manager is to plan and execute the project, to complete it on time and at minimum cost, while meeting or exceeding the required performance of the radar system.

The PTB Simulator is used to train individuals and teams. Individual training focuses on the use of tools and techniques for project planning, monitoring, and control in different situations (scenarios). The Simulator enables a user to experience the efficient and effective use of project management tools and techniques, and to integrate these tools. The traditional method of practicing the use of project management tools is to solve problems in isolation, i.e., without considering all aspects of a particular project plan. For example, to practice project scheduling techniques, a list of project activities is presented along with the estimated duration of each activity and the order in which the activities must be performed. The trainee plots a Gantt chart to estimate the duration of the project and the time each activity should start and finish. This approach is quite efficient in practicing the use of individual tools. However, in practice, integration of different project management tools is frequently required. For example, scheduling decisions depend on the availability of resources that perform the activities and the availability of funds to pay for these resources. Furthermore, due to uncertainty, the exact duration of each activity is not known at the planning stage, and uncertainty or risk may play a major role. As a project progresses, new information is made available and the project plan must be updated accordingly. This integrated, dynamic, and stochastic (uncertain) process is impossible to practice by solving problems manually or by discussing written case studies that represent a snapshot of a project situation. There is a need to see the whole project over a period of time and apply a variety of tools to experience project management complexity. PTB satisfies this need. PTB simulates project execution and informs the user of its outcome. The user can analyze results and decide if and how to change the project plan.

Team training is performed by assigning specific roles to team members. For example, if teams of two are trained, one team member may play the role of a system engineer responsible for the technology decisions while the other team member plays the role of the project manager focusing on the schedule, the budget, and risk management. The team members must develop a shared understanding of the project as technology and business decisions are intertwined. For example, selection of a specific technology for the radar transmitter will impact the cost and duration of transmitter development, as well as performance of the overall radar system.

In advanced courses, both the Scenario Builder and the PTB Simulator are used. A user has to collect information about a real or imaginary project and use the Scenario Builder to develop a scenario based on the data collected. The scenario is used by the PTB Simulator to plan and execute the project.

In the following chapters, different aspects of project management are discussed along with supporting tools and techniques. Each chapter is organized as follows. A discussion on a project management *knowledge area* is followed by the introduction of tools and techniques relevant to that area. These tools and techniques are demonstrated by the PTB Simulator for the scenario that accompanies the software provided with the book.

2.4. Experience in Using PTB

PTB was used in a project management course at the Columbia University School of Engineering. The course focused on project management models and methodologies, for example, the Critical Path Method (CPM). The class was comprised of both full-time undergraduate and graduate engineering students. In addition, there was a section of part-time students who were working while attending school. In general, the students had strong quantitative backgrounds and had taken preliminary courses in linear programming, probability and statistics, and simulation.

In the class, PTB was used by the instructor to illustrate trade-offs that arise in project management. For example, less-expensive resources may be hired in order to reduce the cost of certain project activities. However, the on-time delivery and quality of milestones may suffer. PTB enabled students to measure, through reports and graphs, the trade-offs and to rapidly simulate, and evaluate alternative scenarios.

One course assignment required students to form groups (teams of 2–3 students) and create a project of their own. Some of the project application areas included:

- Manufacturing of consumer products,
- Planning an entertainment or charity event,
- Building construction,
- Information technology/software development,
- New product introduction.

PTB was used to model and simulate each team's project. Students were responsible for identifying data that pertained to their particular project (for example, cost information, resource requirements, etc.). Those students with work experience had an advantage in completing this assignment, as they had first-hand knowledge of a particular application domain. PTB enabled students to efficiently and effectively evaluate various scenarios, based on project duration, project cost, and resource usage.

One example of a student project is the expansion of a sales force by a pharmaceutical company in order to launch and promote a new medicine. The pharmaceutical industry spent $6.5 billion on physician detailing in 2011 (IMS Health, 2012), accounting for 55% of total pharmaceutical industry promotional spending (Martin, 2011). Physician detailing describes the activity in which sales representatives engage physicians in an effort to provide the latest, accurate product information and to encourage them to prescribe the representative's company's products to patients. When a pharmaceutical company launches a new product, building or expanding a sales force to promote the new product is typically the most significant marketing investment. For example, the fully-loaded cost of a 500-person sales force is roughly $125 million per year.

The pharmaceutical industry is highly regulated, requiring significant and specialized training of sales representatives. For example, in the US, the 2010 Physicians Payments Sunshine Act required that sales representatives rely only on data and facts in selling and promoting their products. The landscape is shifting to more of an "evidence-based, therapeutic sell" (Martin, 2011) in which sales representatives need to fully understand the disease state and grasp the science behind the product.

Sizing of sales forces [see Sinha and Zoltners (2001) for a survey of methods] and deployment of sales representatives (i.e., optimal set of physicians to be reached by sales force promotion and the corresponding frequency of the detailing effort) are important management science business problems faced by pharmaceutical companies. Many companies developed statistical, promotion response models that recommend optimal reach and frequency for different physician segments for different products, e.g., see Mizik and Jacobson (2004).

The process for building or expanding an existing sales force in order to launch a new product is complicated and cuts across many commercial departments of a pharmaceutical organization. A project management office is typically required to coordinate the interconnected activities. A high-level project plan would include the following activities:

- Project Approval,
- Sales Force Territory Alignment,
- Customer Targeting,
- Hiring,
- On-Boarding,
- Training,
- Deployment.

Resources are needed from the following functional areas to support the project (Table 2.1).

The most likely duration times in weeks for each activity is provided in Table 2.2.

Table 2.1. Cost per week for each resource type

Resource	Cost per Week (1000's)
Marketing	5
Legal	20
HR	5
Sales management	30
Management science	10
Sales operations	10
IT	5
Sales training	5

Table 2.2. Most likely duration times for each activity

Activity	Most Likely Duration Time
Project approval	4
Sales force territory alignment	4
Customer targeting	2
Hiring	12
On-boarding	1
Training	3
Deployment	1

The key resources required for each activity — outside of the project management office — are listed in Table 2.3:

In the Project Approval activity, the marketing team prepares a business case for senior management, requesting a certain sales force size required to meet its 3–5-year sales forecast. Since sales representatives are the most effective — and the most costly — sales instrument, sales force sizing is a critical decision for the marketing team at the time of a new product launch. As part of this activity, a pharmaceutical company must decide if the new sales representatives will be hired internally or if a Contract Sales Organization (CSO) will be utilized. A CSO strategy mitigates the upfront risk for the pharmaceutical firm. However, the firm has

Table 2.3. Resource requirements for each activity

Activity	No. of Resources Required
Project approval	Marketing — 3 Legal — 2 HR — 1 Sales management — 1
Sales force territory Alignment	Management science — 3 Sales operations — 1
Customer targeting	Management science — 3 Sales operations — 1
Hiring	HR — 5
On-boarding	IT — 8 Sales operations — 3
Training	Sales training — 5 Sales operations — 2
Deployment	Sales management — 1 Sales operations — 2

less control of the people. For example, CSO representatives may promote multiple products that span multiple pharmaceutical companies. The key line organizations that are involved in this activity include a firm's legal and Human Resource (HR) teams. In addition, a firm's business development group will be involved if the firm decides to build its sales force through hiring a third party. Ultimately, senior management must approve the strategy, as a sales force expansion typically involves tens of millions of dollars.

Sales force alignment involves the creation of sales territories. In this activity, the number of sales representatives is determined, and the specific geographies of each sales representative's territory are mapped out. The sales force organization structure is also determined. For example, 8–12 sales representatives will report to a district manager, 6–8 district managers will report to a regional sales director, and 4–6 regional directors will report to a national sales Vice President (VP) who is located in company headquarters. The creation of a sales force alignment and structure is a classic management science business problem in the pharmaceutical industry. Ideally, sales territories should be "balanced" with each sales territory containing roughly the same level of workload. Territory workload is measured by considering the potential number of customers in the territory weighted by the desired frequency that each customer will be called on by a sales representative. In addition to workload balance, the size of the territory and the geographic boundaries of the territory are important considerations. A large territory that encompasses significant rural areas may be inefficient, as it would require significant travel time. In some cases, a company may choose to leave certain rural areas uncovered due to the lack of customer density. Geographic boundaries also figure into decision making, as territories and districts should obey county and state borders. In the pharmaceutical industry, managed health care plans vary by state in the US. If a sales territory can be contained in one state — rather than crossing into multiple states — it lessens the training that the sales representative requires with respect to understanding and keeping current with arcane, state-managed care policies.

The activity of customer (i.e., physician or health care provider) target selection complements the sales force territory alignment activity. Both tasks are typically managed and performed by the pharmaceutical company's management science department. In customer target selection, each territory is assigned a list of targets. Some targets may not be unique to a particular territory, as some doctors have multiple offices, spread across two or more territories. Each territory's capacity is measured by the number of calls that a sales representative may execute, on average, each day. The average number of calls per day may vary by geography, i.e., it may increase in dense population areas and it may decrease in sparse population areas. An optimal number of calls per time period (e.g., per quarter) must be determined. Call frequency will vary, based on the sales potential of each customer in the territory. A territory with a relatively high number of valuable customers will, therefore, have fewer customer targets than a territory with a relatively low number of valuable customers, since valuable customers will be called on more frequently.

The HR group plays a vital role in building or expanding a sales force. New representatives must be recruited and hired. A hiring profile must first be developed. In this step, the HR department, in conjunction with the marketing and sales organizations, determines the ideal profile of a sales representative candidate (e.g., minimum and maximum prior experience in pharmaceutical sales). Positions must be posted and shared with appropriate recruiters. Positions can only be posted upon completion of the territory alignment task, since a sales representative candidate must be informed of the exact geographic specifications of the sales territory for which he or she is applying. In some cases, a firm will require that each sales representative reside in the sales territory that they support. Candidates must be interviewed by district managers, and employment offers must be prepared and extended. Once background checks are completed, a complete roster of sales representatives may be presented.

Once a roster of sales representatives is created in the hiring task, the on-boarding activity may commence. In this activity, sales representatives are provided with hardware, software, and other physical assets, such as a car and sales material, that they will need to execute their assignments. A company's Information Technology (IT) and operations groups are the critical resources needed to execute this activity. Sales representatives are usually on the road. They carry laptops and mobile devices to access customer data. Most major pharmaceutical companies utilize Sales Force Automation (SFA) software that allows a sales representative to log physician calls and distribution of product samples. As pointed out above, the pharmaceutical industry is highly regulated, and rules governing the distribution of product samples are strictly enforced. The on-boarding activity is complete when all sales representatives receive their hardware shipments, software access, and automobile fleet assignments.

Training is a critical task in the project and requires completion of the on-boarding activity. Sales representatives are trained through both remote and live training sessions. On-line training ("home study") can take place once a sales representative receives hardware and software. On-line training is often complemented by live training whereby a critical mass of new sales representatives gather in a central location to be trained by a live trainer. Various sub-tasks must be coordinated in order for live training to take place: training site selection, a trainer or trainers, travel arrangements to enable the sales representatives to travel to the training site, and finally, training materials. As noted above, pharmaceutical sales representatives engage a scientific, knowledgeable customer base — physicians and health care providers. Sales representatives must be trained in the "science" of the products that they sell in order to be credible and effective.

The training activity concludes with certification. In essence, sales representatives must pass certain tests and establish proficiency with respect to the products that they will be promoting. Once these tests are successfully completed, a sales representative may be deployed in the field, promoting the company's launch product.

Deployment of sales representatives is the final, major activity of the overall project. A regional or national sales meeting can often precede the actual, field deployment. A kickoff meeting, chaired by either the sales VP or a regional sales director, serves to emphasize the goals of the sales campaign and energize the sales representatives. In addition, certain training modules can be repeated and re-enacted, e.g., role-playing exercises. If a sales meeting is held as part of the deployment activity, logistics for the meeting (program agenda, meeting location, travel, food and lodging, audio/visual equipment) must be coordinated. As part of the deployment activity, each sales representative is presented with a customer target list and any data regarding the customers. This activity and the overall project are completed, once the sales representatives begin their first day of physician detailing.

There are two opportunities to compress the time duration required to complete the project. Specifically, the Territory Alignment and Targeting activities may be expedited, for example, additional or more experienced Management Science resources can be deployed on the Territory Alignment activity.

The process of assembling a sales force to support the launch of a pharmaceutical product involves a complex set of activities involving multiple disciplines in a pharmaceutical company: marketing, sales, HR, management science, IT, training, legal, and operations. A project management office is typically responsible for coordinating the different activities and functions. The project management team — which may be external to the pharmaceutical company — will rely on a number of internal champions. Often, a member of the operations team will coordinate functions such as management science, IT, etc., bringing in those resources at key points in the project when they are needed and then releasing those resources after their particular function is completed.

A product launch is critical to a product's ultimate success in the marketplace. A successful and effective sales force development and deployment plan is critical to a product launch.

2.5. The PTB Main Screens and Commands

The PTB is a project management simulator designed for teaching project management and training project managers and their teams in using the tools and techniques of project management.

The user has to plan a project and control its execution. The project is considered complete when each task has been planned, processed, and executed. The user's goal is to minimize waste and maximize the value of the project, including maximizing the delivered system's benefit at the end of the project.

Each project has a due date. In the case of a late completion of a project, a penalty may be charged. The penalty is calculated per period and is added to the project cost. The penalty may represent the opportunity cost due to delayed time to market, or a real penalty based on a contract with a customer. Late completion will occur if the project continues past the due date; this is usually due to the uncertainty in the project environment as well as a poorly planned or poorly executed project or both. In the case of early completion, a bonus (per period) may be added to the project cash flow.

The simulator includes predefined projects (scenarios) that the user has to plan and execute. Some (easy) scenarios are deterministic. In these scenarios, the execution of the project is performed exactly according to the plan. There are also stochastic scenarios. In the stochastic scenarios, there is uncertainty regarding the duration and cost of the tasks and/or the availability of resources. Due to this uncertainty, the actual duration, the actual costs and the actual availability of resources may differ from the original plan.

2.5.1. *Getting started*

The PTB is web-based. To use PTB, you must use the unique code provided with the book.

1. Using **Internet Explorer** from a Windows computer, connect to http://www.sandboxmodel.com/ and select "Run It" and "Run the student version of PTB" in the sub-menu.
2. Press the "Run the latest version of the PTB Simulator" link.
3. If prompted by the browser, continue the launch of the program by selecting "allow" or "yes" as needed.

Fig. 2.3. PTB opening screen

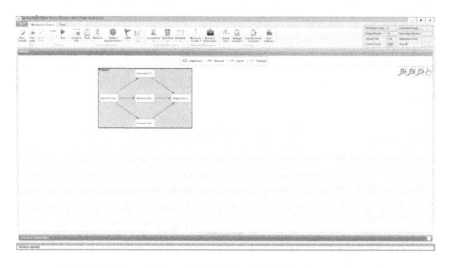

Fig. 2.4. Network view of the Medium Radar Development scenario

4. Once the software starts, log in using your username and password. When the PTB starts, the **Opening Screen** is presented (see Fig. 2.3).

The user has to enter a user name and a password, to read and accept the license agreement, and to click on OK to start using PTB.

Next, the network view of the **Medium Radar Development** scenario opens up on the screen (see Fig. 2.4).

Once the scenario is opened and during the scenario run, detailed information on the scenario is available by pressing the "Further Scenario

Fig. 2.5. Further Scenario Information

Fig. 2.6. The magnifier buttons

Information" button under the "View" menu group, in the "Tools" menu tab as illustrated in Fig. 2.5.

A user may zoom in or out by clicking on the magnifier buttons on the upper right side of the screen where the project network is displayed (see Fig. 2.6).

2.6. Information

At different time points during the simulation, different views are available to supply information about the scenario.

2.6.1. *Basic information*

Some basic scenario information is presented on the upper right corner of the screen (see Fig. 2.7):

Simulation Time	0	Estimated Cash	
Target Period	15	Estimated Period	
Target Cost	41K	Estimated Cost	
Current Cash	100K	Benefit	

Fig. 2.7. Basic scenario information

The basic scenario information includes:

- **Simulation Time** — The current simulation time (time = 0 at the start of the simulation). Each time the simulation is run, the current simulation time is advanced by at least one time period (the user may choose to run several time periods in each run).
- **Target Period** — The project due date. The objective is to run the simulation and complete the project within this number of periods.
- **Target Cost** — The desired project cost. The objective is to complete the project at a cost not higher than the target cost.
- **Current Cash** — The cash position at the current simulation time.
- **Estimated Cash** — The estimated cash position at the end of the project. This is calculated as the initial cash position minus the estimated cost plus the expected income associated with completing the project.
- **Estimated Period** — The expected time to finish the simulated project according to the current plan (presented only after the project is planned).
- **Estimated Cost** — The expected cost of the project according to the current plan (presented only after the project is planned).
- **Benefit** — The expected benefit (or value to stakeholders) of the project according to the current plan. Benefit measures the performance of the system delivered by the project or how well it satisfies system requirements.

2.6.2. *Information menu*

Information regarding the project is available through the General Information, Financial Information, and Resource Information menu groups under the "Plan Execute Control" menu tab (see Fig. 2.8). Some information is available once a Scenario is opened, and the balance is only available after the Scenario has been planned.

Fig. 2.8.   Plan Execute Control menu tab

2.6.3. *Preplanning information*

Along with the Network view, three views can be presented in the lower part of the screen before the project is planned: scenario information, task information, and resource information.

2.6.4. *Network view*

By clicking on the Network button under the "General Information" menu group in the "Plan Execute Control" menu tab, the network is presented in the upper portion of the screen. Each node represents a task, and the arcs represent precedence relations between tasks. The color of each node represents the status of the corresponding task.

- A blue border represents a task that is not yet planned, i.e., the task start time and the task mode are not yet selected.
- A blue stripe represents a task that is planned but has not started, i.e., the task start time and the task mode of operation have been defined.
- A half-orange half-blue stripe represents a task that is planned and started but not yet finished.
- An orange stripe represents a task that is completed. (see Fig. 2.9):

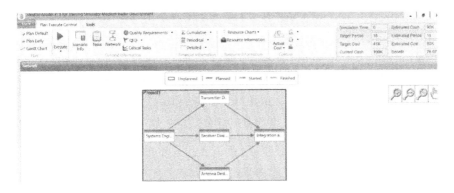

Fig. 2.9. The network view and the network legend

2.6.5. Scenario information

Clicking on the Scenario Info button, under the "General Information" menu group in the "Plan Execute Control" menu tab, opens the Scenario Information screen which includes the following information for each project (see Fig. 2.10):

- **Project Name** — The unique name assigned to the project.
- **Number of Tasks** — The number of tasks the project contains.
- **Target Date** — The project's required duration (assuming that the project starts in period zero). One of the goals is to finish running the simulation within this number of periods.
- **Initial Cash** — The amount of cash available at the beginning of the project.
- **Target Cost** — The desired project cost. The objective is to complete the project at a cost not higher than the target cost.
- **Bonus/Period** — The bonus per period in case of early completion of the project. The bonus is awarded for each period that the project is completed before the Target Date.
- **Penalty/Period** — The penalty per period in case of late completion of the project. The penalty has to be paid for each period in which the project is still not completed after the Target Date.
- **Systems Engineering Enabled** — Indicates that specific requirements are defined for the project and the user has to plan the project to achieve these requirements.

2.6.6. Task information

Information regarding the project tasks and the precedence relations among project tasks is presented by pressing the Tasks button under the General Information menu group in the "Plan Execute Control" menu

Project Name	Number of Tasks	Target Date	Initial Cash	Target Cost	Bonus per Period	Penalty per Period	System Engineering Enabled
Project1	5	15	100000	41000	10000	20000	True

Fig. 2.10.   Scenario information

Project Name	Task Name	Predecessors
Project1	Systems Engineering	
Project1	Transmitter Design	Systems Engineering
Project1	Receiver Design	Systems Engineering
Project1	Antenna Design	Systems Engineering
Project1	Integration and Testing	Transmitter Design,Receiver Design,Antenna Design

Fig. 2.11. Task information

Name	Available Units	Units Available in Lead Time	Cost/Period	Idle Cost/Period	Releasing Cost	Assigning Cost	Show Up Probability (%)	Releasing Lead Time	Assigning Lead Time	Minimum Units	Maximum
Engineers	20	20	100	50	50	50	80	1		1	30
Technicians	20	20	50	10	40	20	85	1		2	50

Select Resource [　　　▾] Release [1] Units Assign [1] Units

Fig. 2.12. Resource information

tab (see Fig. 2.11). This table presents the tasks of each project listed by project name, task name, and a list of predecessor tasks. The precedence relations in the simulator are finish to start; that is, if task X is a predecessor to task Y, then task X must be finished before task Y can start.

2.6.7. *Resource information*

Resource information is presented in the lower part of the screen by pressing the Resource Information button under the Resource Information menu group in the "Plan Execute Control" menu tab (see Fig. 2.12).

The resource information is summarized in a table that includes the following data:

- **Name** — The name of the resource type.
- **Available Units** — The available quantity of the resource at the current time.
- **Units Available in Lead Time** — The quantity of the resource that will be available after the assign and release lead time elapses.

- **Cost per Period** — Per period cost of the resource. This is the cost while the resource is assigned to a task.
- **Idle Cost per Period** — Per period cost of the resource while not performing a task.
- **Releasing Cost** — The cost of reducing a resource availability by one unit (if it is an income this number will be negative).
- **Assigning Cost** — The cost of increasing a resource's availability by one unit.
- **Show up Probability (%)** — The probability that a resource unit will be available to work on the project's tasks in any given period (displayed as a percentage). If, for example, the Show up Probability is 95%, then there is a 5% chance that each resource unit of this type will not be available in a specific time period.
- **Releasing Lead Time** — The amount of time (time periods) required to release a resource unit.
- **Assigning Lead Time** — The amount of time (time periods) required to assign a resource unit.
- **Minimum Units** — The minimum number of resource units the user can use.
- **Maximum Units** — The maximum number of resource units the user can use.

Some resource and financial information is available only after the project tasks are planned, i.e., a mode is selected and a starting time is assigned. These reports and metrics are covered in later chapters.

2.7. Summary

The need to train project managers and project teams and to teach students how to manage projects motivated the development of SBT platforms. These platforms provide hands-on experience in using the tools and techniques of project management without incurring the risks associated with making the wrong decisions. The PTB Simulator is unique, as it can simulate any kind of project with various levels of complexity and uncertainty. The student version of PTB, provided with this book, includes three project scenarios, of varying complexity, that provide an opportunity to apply project management tools and techniques.

References

IMS Health (2012). Private communication.

Kasser, J. E., John, P., Tipping, K. and Yeoh, L. W. (2008). Systems engineering a 21st century introductory course on systems engineering: The Seraswati Project, *Proceedings of the 2nd Asia Pacific Conference on Systems Engineering*, Yokohama, Japan.

Martin, C. (2011). Pharmaceutical sales reps of the future, www.capstrat.com.

Mizik, N. and Jacobson, R. (2004). Are physicians 'easy marks'? Quantifying the effects of detailing and sampling on new prescriptions, *Management Science*, **50**(12), pp. 1704–1715.

Murray, H. J. R. (2015). *A History of Chess: The Original 1913 Edition*. Skyhorse Publishing, Inc., New York.

Sinha, P. and Zoltners, A. A. (2001). Sales-force decision models: Insights from 25 years of implementation, *Interfaces*, 31, pp. S8–S44.

Chapter 3

Stakeholder Requirements and Value

3.1. Who are the Stakeholders?

Projects are performed to create value. Value is created by satisfying the needs and expectations of project stakeholders. Project management focuses on an effort to maximize value while minimizing waste, i.e., minimizing the time, effort, and funds spent on non-value-added activities.

A project stakeholder may be either an individual or an organization. Examples include:

- Customers
- Users
- The project sponsor (who funds the project)
- Shareholders
- The project team members
- Managers of the organization performing the project
- Subcontractors
- Suppliers

Some stakeholders are primarily concerned with the underlying business problem that is being addressed by the project. Other stakeholders focus on the methodology and approach to solving the business problem. Stakeholders have different levels of influence on project success. Some stakeholders are judges — they will decide if the project is successful or not upon its completion. For example, although the Opera House in Sydney was delayed in its completion, it was judged by the public — a key stakeholder group — to be a huge success (based on the number of visitors per year). Some stakeholders can impact the project during its planning and/or during its execution. A typical example is the project sponsor who provides funding and can terminate the project prematurely if it fails to achieve its objectives. A regulator is also a stakeholder, as it can shut down a project if laws or regulations are violated.

From the above examples, it is clear that stakeholders can be mapped to several dimensions:

- **Influence** — The extent to which a stakeholder is able to act on project/program planning or operations and therefore affect project/program outcomes.
- **Importance** — The extent to which a stakeholder's interests, expectations, and requirements are affected by project/program outcomes.
- **Engagement** — A measure of how well the stakeholder understands the challenges the project seeks to tackle and the project's interests, expectations, and requirements.
- **Commitment** — A measure of investment of time, money, equipment, facilities, or personnel.

The project manager has to identify and map the stakeholders and, based on the mapping, decide how to interact with each of them. Some possible policies are:

Partner
Key stakeholders with high influence and high importance to project success are likely to provide the basis of the project's "coalition of support" and are potential *partners* in planning and implementation.

Consult
A key stakeholder who is aware of a program or project — but low on commitment — can be a significant risk if not properly managed. To increase such a stakeholder's commitment, a project manager can solicit his/her opinion or advice prior to major program decisions.

Inform
For key stakeholders who are high on commitment but low on engagement, increasing the quality, quantity, or timeliness of information would be helpful to moving them toward being program advocates.

Monitor
For stakeholders with low engagement and low involvement, the best approach is to "monitor" their input — to ensure that project resources are not diverted.

3.2. From Needs and Expectations to Product Scope

A project manager is responsible for translating stakeholders' needs and expectations into project goals (products and/or services that must be delivered by the project) and project constraints that cannot be violated. When project needs and expectations are defined, a project team can propose efficient and effective feasible solutions that do not violate constraints. Typical project goals involve the performance and quality of project deliverables, timely completion of the project, and minimizing the project cost. Collectively, performance/quality, schedule, and cost are known as the project triangle. Each of these may have an associated constraint. For example, a product or service must achieve a threshold quality standard. Otherwise, the project is a failure, regardless of its duration and cost. Other examples of project constraints are a maximum acceptable project duration time and a maximum available budget.

During project initiation, alternative configurations are developed and analyzed. Each configuration describes the feature and functions of the end deliverable (product, service, or system). Configuration selection is based on the expected performance, quality, schedule duration, cost, and the level of risk associated with each configuration. For example, in the radar development scenario described in Chapter 2, one configuration is based on purchasing the whole radar system off the shelf; a second configuration is based on a radar system with two antennas — a transmitting antenna and a receiving antenna; and a third configuration is a radar system with a single antenna that transmits and receives electromagnetic waves. Each configuration has its pros and cons. The process of selecting an alternative among candidate proposals is discussed in Chapter 1.

3.3. The Sales Force Expansion Project

The sales force expansion project, introduced in Chapter 2, serves as an example to illustrate how the differing objectives and perspectives of different stakeholder groups must be balanced and managed by a project manager. In this example, the marketing team is primarily interested in maximizing product sales. The product brand team's bonuses and incentives are, typically, driven by the number of units sold in the first year following product launch. These stakeholders, therefore, are interested in building as large a sales force as possible, since more sales representatives will lead to increased sales. On the other hand, senior management — which typically includes an organization's Chief Financial Officer (CFO) — is primarily concerned with profitability. Although these stakeholders are, of course, interested in maximizing top-line revenue, their desire to manage the cost side and limit the organization's financial risk is paramount.

In addition to the natural tension between marketing (emphasizing top-line revenue and striving for maximal sales force expansion) and senior management/finance (emphasizing bottom-line costs and seeking to limit sales force expansion), there are other significant stakeholders whose positions must be considered. For example, the sales representatives themselves would like to work sales territories that are dense with potential sales opportunities. A sales representative is interested in maximizing engagement time with customers and minimizing travel time. Sales representatives, in general, prefer geographically dense territories in order to maximize customer sales calls per day.

The training group also has certain desires with respect to building a sales force and launching a new product. Sales representatives must be properly trained in the product's profile and be fully knowledgeable regarding the product's efficacy and safety. A sales representative must be trained on a product's position in its market; that is, the strengths and weaknesses of a product relative to its competition. In the US pharmaceutical industry, training is of extreme importance. Messaging and marketing materials are approved by the US Food and Drug Administration (FDA), and a sales representative is constrained, by law, to follow a specific selling protocol. Training must, therefore, be thorough, and sales representatives must pass certain, internal, tests before they are permitted to go into the field and engage customers. Training requirements are, at times, at odds with marketing (who seek to begin product promotion as soon as possible) and finance (who seek to minimize expenditures).

A project manager's responsibility is to engage each of the stakeholder groups and draw out their objectives and constraints. The project manager must, typically, conduct a negotiation process in which stakeholders are brought together to find acceptable compromise solutions. In some organizations, a decision-making culture of consensus building is required. In such a culture, a project manager must arrive at a business solution that is acceptable to all key parties. In other organizational cultures, alternative decision-making processes may govern; for example, (i) majority rule or (ii) a particular line organization is given both decision-making responsibility and accountability. In the sales force expansion project, the marketing organization may be given the ultimate decision-making power on sizing a new sales force, since marketing is the organization with which the sales force is most closely involved. However, in such a culture, the marketing organization will also be held accountable if the sales force does not deliver the top-line revenue that was forecast.

3.4. From Product Scope to Project Scope

The result of the stakeholders' analysis is a plan for satisfying each set of stakeholder needs and expectations. As we saw in the sales force expansion project, conflicting needs and expectations must be addressed and the project manager (and the project management team) must decide on the project work content (the project scope) and the specifications of the project deliverables (the product scope). This decision may be decomposed into a hierarchy with several levels. Consider the radar system development example introduced in Chapter 2. At the top level, the decision is whether to develop a new radar system (the go/no go decision which involves portfolio management). At the next level, if the first decision is a "go", alternative technologies might be considered for each (major) component of the radar system. For example, it might be possible to modify an existing transmitter based on well-known technology or to develop a new transmitter based on cutting-edge new technology. This decision may impact not only the transmitter power, quality, and reliability, but also project time duration, cost and required resources.

Several tools and methodologies support scope management. One example is requirements management. Each requirement is defined precisely, if possible with a specific formula or equation; a minimum threshold value and acceptable range for that performance measure are also specified.

In the radar development example, one requirement is the desired radar range: the maximum distance from which the radar system can detect an airplane. The radar range is a function of the transmitter power, the receiver sensitivity, and the antenna gain. The project manager and team may define a minimum acceptable range (say, 10 miles), but the range, desired by key stakeholders, is 12 miles. In general, the better systems have higher ranges.

In order to achieve the desired range, the design of the transmitter, the receiver, and the antenna should be coordinated, based on the radar equation. Ideally, the desired range is achieved while satisfying a maximum project duration constraint, without exceeding project budget, and taking into account other risk, quality, and reliability requirements.

In the next section, the tools built into the Project Team Builder to support scope management are discussed.

3.5. Value and Scope in the PTB

In the PTB simulator, a stakeholder's needs and expectations are translated into system requirements. System requirements define the performance or quality goals and constraints imposed on the deliverables of the project. In order to best follow the description below, the user is advised to click the Plan Default button. Following that step, the user should click on the Run button, which is a dropdown option after clicking on the Execute button on the main tab. In order to align with the discussion below, it is suggested that the scenario be run for 19 periods (using the Run feature). The scenario will run till the form "Scenario Finished, Summary" will pop up. Click on Ok at the bottom of this form.

The Quality Requirements icon is located in the general information menu (see Fig. 3.1).

Clicking on the Quality Requirements button displays the list of requirements for the project deliveries. Each row of the Quality Requirements list represents a requirement. The range of values for the requirement, its relative weight, and the formula (equation) by which the requirement is calculated are displayed (see Fig. 3.2 for the radar development scenario default plan).

The entries in the Quality Requirements list specify the following for the project deliverables:

The **Name** of each requirement, e.g., Range or Quality.

The **Formula** (equation) by which the specific value of the requirement is calculated for a specific design (or project plan).

The **Importance** is a weight or relative importance of the requirement in calculating the value generated by the design (or project plan).

The **Minimum Value** acceptable for this requirement if the goal is to maximize.

The **Desired Value** or target value for this requirement.

Fig. 3.1. Quality Requirements button

Name	Formula	Importance	Minimum Value	Desired Value	Maximum Value	Best Mode	Evaluation	Project	Score
∧ Project1									
Range	POWER([TP]*[RS]*[AG]0.25)	7	10	12	NA	Maximum	11.07	Project1	53.5
Quality	[SEQ]*[QT]*[QR]*[QA]*[QI]*100	8	0	75	NA	Maximum	59.59	Project1	79.45
Reliability	[AR]*[IR]*[TR]*[RR]*100	6	0	65	NA	Maximum	65.61	Project1	100

Fig. 3.2. System Requirements list

The **Maximum Value** acceptable for this requirement if the goal is to minimize.

The **Best Mode** is the goal — to minimize or maximize the value of this requirement.

The **Evaluation** for the current design. The evaluation value is color coded. If the evaluation value is green, the value for this requirement is in the allowable range (i.e., between the acceptable minimum and desired value if we try to maximize, and between the desired value and the acceptable maximum if we try to minimize). If the evaluation value is orange, the value for this requirement is better than the desired value (i.e., above the desired value if we try to maximize, and below the desired value if we try to minimize). An orange color represents overdesign or gold-plating. If the evaluation value is red, the value for this requirement is worse than the accepted value (i.e., below the accepted minimum if we try to maximize, and above the accepted maximum if we try to minimize). In other words, a red evaluation indicates an infeasible plan with respect to the requirement. In order for the overall design to be feasible, all requirements must be either green or orange — even a single requirement being red will cause a design to become infeasible.

The **Score** of each requirement is based on its evaluation. The score is a number between 0 and 100. Its calculation is described below.

Quality Requirement evaluations are calculated based on the modes selected for the project activities (tasks). Each parameter in the formula is set by selecting a mode of a project task. For example, the parameter Transmitter Power (TP) is set by the mode of the task Transmitter Design. This task has two modes of execution: Reengineer and New Design. If the task is performed in the Reengineer mode, then TP will get a value of 50. On the other hand, if the New Design mode is selected, TP will get a value of 100 (see Fig. 3.3). Figure 3.3 is generated by clicking on the Gantt chart button and then clicking on the Transmitter Design bar. Since TP is a quality parameter in the Range Requirement Formula, changing its value will affect the evaluation of the Range.

To see which tasks include quality parameters that affect a specific system requirement, the user can move the mouse over to the specific formula under Quality Requirements (see Fig. 3.4).

The same information can be viewed by clicking the QFD button (see Fig. 3.5).

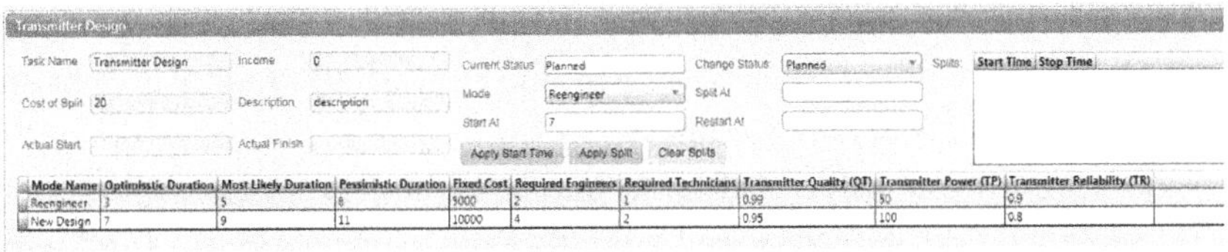

Fig. 3.3. Value of the quality parameter in a single mode task

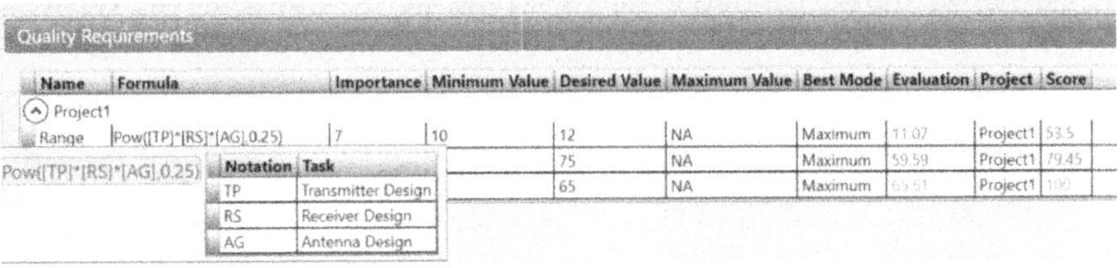

Fig. 3.4. List of tasks that affect system requirement evaluation

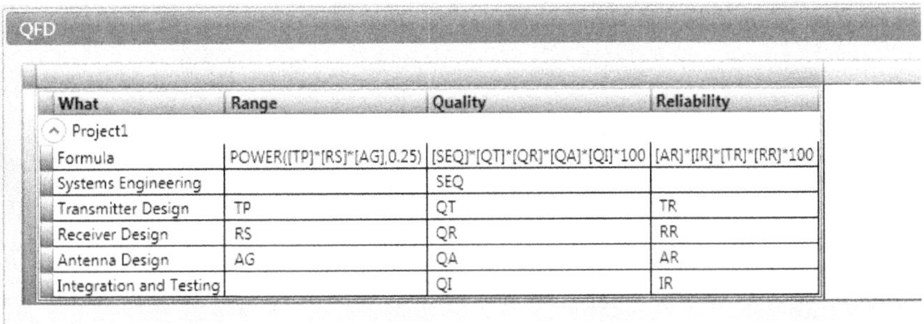

Fig. 3.5. QFD View

When the project tasks are planned and a mode is selected for each task, the PTB evaluates and presents the values selected for the parameters and the calculated value (evaluation) of each requirement, as shown in Fig. 3.2. The selection of modes affects the cost, the resource requirements, the task duration, and the system (quality) requirements. At the end of the PTB run, the total benefit and the total cost of the scenario are calculated and displayed as a basis for cost–benefit analysis. The total benefit is calculated as follows:

Each requirement is assigned an importance value or weight between 1 and 10 according to its relative importance to stakeholders. For example, in Fig. 3.4, the importance of the radar range is set to 7. These weights are normalized by dividing each weight by the sum of all weights to obtain normalized weights between 0 and 1.

Each requirement is evaluated and assigned an evaluation score between 0 and 100. This is done by interpolation (using a linear function) between the points of desired value for the requirement (evaluation score of 100) and the acceptable value for the requirement (evaluation score of 0). For example, the radar range should be maximized. The desired value is 12 miles, and the minimum value is 10 miles. If the evaluated value based on the formula and modes selected for transmitter design, receiver design, and antenna design is 11, then the evaluation score is calculated by interpolation as:

$$(11-10)*[(100-0)/(12-10)] = 50.$$

Similarly, the range evaluation of 11.07 in Fig. 3.4 is translated to a score of

$$(11.07-10)*[(100-0)/(12-10)] = 53.5.$$

In case the required value is to be minimized, the desired value will be assigned a score of 100, while the maximum acceptable value will be assigned a score of 0.

The benefit or value of the whole system is calculated as a weighted sum of the system requirement evaluations. The benefit is calculated by summing up, for all system requirements, the scores multiplied by the normalized weight of each requirement; the benefit value is presented in the dashboard at the upper right corner of the screen and in a short summary report at the end of the simulation run (see Fig. 3.6).

In the upper portion of Fig. 3.6, the final report generated after each run is presented along with the system requirements table. The benefit of the system at the end of the run is 76.67. This is calculated as follows:

$$[7/(7+8+6)]53.5 + [8/(7+8+6)]79.45 + [6/(7+8+6)]100 = 76.67.$$

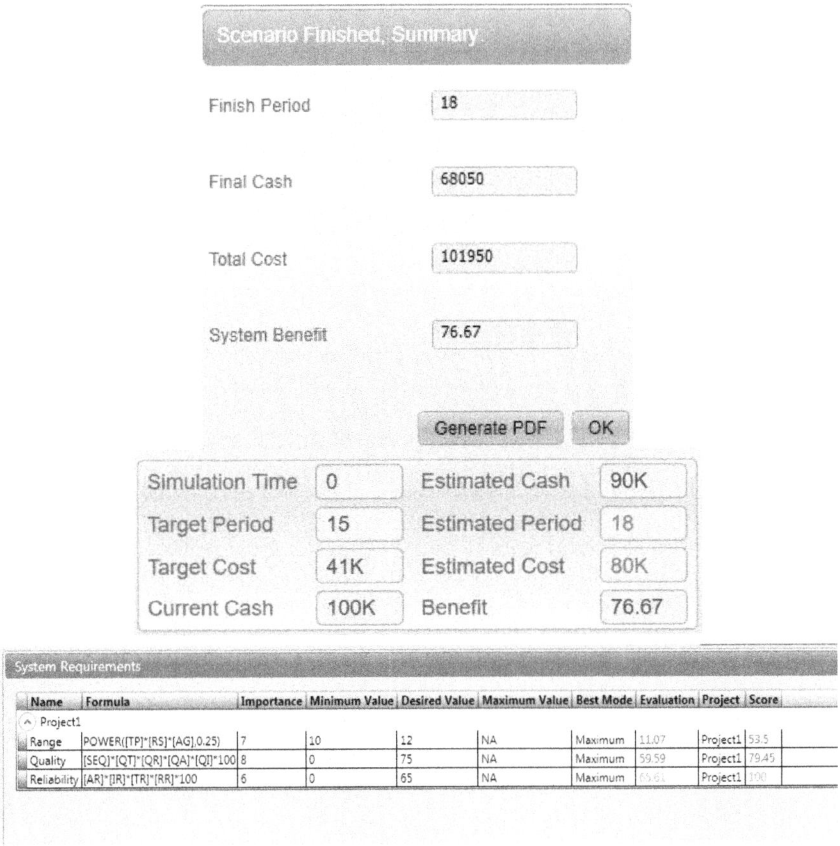

Fig. 3.6. Evaluation of the system requirements for the default design

3.6. Summary

The translation of stakeholder needs and expectations into a project scope and a product scope is a necessary step in project management. Stakeholder analysis, requirements analysis, and a clear definition of value are valuable tools in this process. PTB supports scope management by making these tools easily available to the user who can evaluate the benefits and shortfalls of different scenarios.

Chapter 4

Scheduling

4.1. What is a Schedule and Why is It Needed?

The Oxford dictionary defines a schedule as "a plan for carrying out a process or procedure, giving lists of intended events and times". Schedules are important for the coordination of efforts of resources working together on the same project to achieve its specific goals. The schedule defines what should be done and when it should be done. Based on the schedule, resources can be made available in a timely fashion. Resource scheduling is particularly important when the availability of resources is limited. In such cases, resources may need to be ordered or planned for weeks, months, or even years in advance. When resources need to be planned for in advance of when they are needed by a project, we refer to the resource as having a long lead time. For example, ordering a piece of equipment like a turbine in a power plant, rare materials, or a person with very special skills may often be associated with a long lead time. A schedule is a list of tasks (or activities) and the planned start and end time of these tasks. More information may be presented on a schedule, such as the resources needed to perform each task or special events called milestones.

1. Preparing the Schedule — Tools and Techniques

There are different kinds of schedules that can be prepared based on the needs of the project stakeholders and the project characteristics. Some scheduling tools are deterministic — assuming that the level of uncertainty is low enough to be ignored. Other tools take uncertainty into account and analyze its impact on the project. In this section, we discuss three commonly used scheduling tools — the Gantt chart and the Critical Path Method (CPM) — that ignore uncertainty, and Monte Carlo simulation that accounts for uncertainty associated with the duration times of activities.

The Gantt chart — Developed in the early 20th century, a Gantt chart is a graphical tool that presents project activities versus a timeline. Each activity is represented by a bar that spans the time between the planned start and the planned end dates of the activity. This is illustrated in Fig. 4.1

In Fig. 4.1, the five activities of the radar development project, introduced in Chapter 2, are scheduled on a Gantt chart. The schedule in Fig. 4.1 is based on an After Receiving Order (ARO) time scale. The ARO starts at time 0, and the time axis (the horizontal axis) represents working periods (days, weeks, months, etc.). Some Gantt charts use a calendar time scale with a specific start date and note specific holiday weekends, etc. along the horizontal axis. It is convenient to use ARO early on when it is not known yet when the project will start and to change to a calendar when the project start date is decided and the specific calendar that will be used is known.

The Gantt chart takes into account the following data:

• The list of activities,
• The precedence relations among activities,
• The estimated duration of each activity.

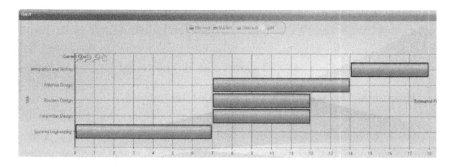

Fig. 4.1. The Gantt chart of the radar development project

This information for the radar development example, presented in Fig. 4.1, is summarized in Table 4.1.

Other information, like the availability of resources and funds, uncertainty, and the impact of resource assignment on the duration of activities, is not used in the construction of a Gantt chart. Therefore, the schedule based on the Gantt chart may not be feasible due to lack of resources, lack of funds, etc. Because of its simplicity, the Gantt chart is widely used for scheduling and for the presentation of schedules developed by other techniques that will be discussed later.

The Critical Path Method — Developed in the late 1950s, the CPM is a mathematical programming model that is frequently presented as a network, as illustrated in Fig. 4.2.

Table 4.1. Information for the radar development example

Activity Name	Activity Duration	Predecessors
Systems engineering	7	—
Transmitter design	5	Systems engineering
Receiver design	5	Systems engineering
Antenna design	7	Systems engineering
Integration and testing	4	Transmitter design, Receiver design, Antenna design

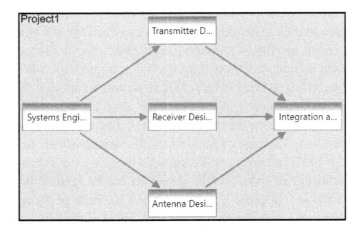

Fig. 4.2. Network of the radar development project

In the network model, each node corresponds to a project activity, and the precedence relations are depicted by arrows. An activity corresponds to the bottom-most tier of a Work Breakdown Structure (WBS) hierarchy. Activities are interrelated by *precedence constraints*. A precedence constraint arises due to a fundamental or technical aspect involving two or more activities. For example, printing a program for a theatrical production can only occur after the cast has been selected.

A project manager should verify precedence constraints with the assistance of subject-matter experts, if necessary. A project manager will encounter many precedence constraints that are offered or suggested by project team members or project stakeholders; for example, only a certain individual developer has the skill set to develop a certain module of software code. A project manager must validate, within a certain high level of confidence, that each precedence constraint holds. In some cases, a project manager can effectively circumvent a precedence constraint through innovative ideas (develop a "Plan B"). By minimizing the impact of precedence constraints — particularly those that impact the critical path (discussed below) — a project manager can reduce project duration and costs and potentially increase project revenues. A project manager's ability to "break" a precedence constraint is dependent on both technical understanding of the underlying engineering and science involved in the affected activities as well as business acumen involved in negotiating requirements and resources with stakeholders and senior management.

Each arrow in the project network represents precedence relations between two activities, starting at the predecessor activity and terminating at the successor activity. A duration time is estimated for each task. For now, we will assume that these duration times are deterministic (known with 100% certainty). Later in this chapter, we will complicate the scheduling problem by assuming that the duration times are stochastic (that is, they are variable, and the variability must be explicitly considered by the project manager). Although duration times of a project task are never truly known with 100% certainty, a task's duration time may, nevertheless, have a tight confidence interval, and the variability can be ignored for project planning purposes. In general, if a similar task has been performed in the past by the same organization and the variability of the task's duration time is negligible, then modeling the duration time as being deterministic is appropriate in practice.

The longest sequence of activities connecting the start of the project to its end is the critical path. The critical path determines the project duration, and the activities on the critical path are called critical activities. The minimum duration of the project is the sum of the durations of the activities on the critical path. Non-critical activities can be delayed without delaying the project. The amount of time a non-critical activity can be delayed without delaying the project is called the slack of the activity. In the radar development example when using the Default Plan in the PTB tool, there are three sequences connecting the start of the project to its end:

(1) The sequence system engineering, Transmitter design, and Integration and testing with a total duration of 16 periods.
(2) The sequence system engineering, receiver design, and Integration and testing with a total duration of 16 periods.
(3) The sequence system engineering, Antenna design, and Integration and testing with a total duration of 18 periods.

The critical activities, when using the Default Plan in the PTB tool, are therefore Systems Engineering, Antenna Design, and Integration and Testing. The activities Transmitter Design and Receiver Design are not critical and can be delayed by two periods each without delaying the project. Thus, the slack of these activities is two periods.

CPM relies on a two-pass algorithm to calculate the earliest and latest start times and finish times of each activity and, thereby, calculate, the minimum project duration. In this example, we assume that there is a single start node with a duration of 0 and a single end node with a duration of 0. In the forward pass, the algorithm assumes that every activity starts as soon as possible; that is, as soon as the last of its predecessor activities is completed. Therefore, the early start (ES) time of an activity is equal to the maximum early finish (EF) times of all of its predecessor activities. The ES of the start node assuming ARO is 0. The EF of an activity is equal to its ES plus its duration.

In the backward pass of the algorithm, the latest start (LS) times and latest finish (LF) times of each activity are calculated. Since the duration time of the End milestone is assumed to be 0, $LF_{END} = EF_{END}$. The backward pass (as its name implies) begins with the End milestone node and works backward through the project network. In general, the LF of an activity is equal to the earliest LS times of all of its successor activities. The LS time of an activity is calculated by its LF less its duration time.

The project network in Fig. 4.3 is used to illustrate the CPM. As shown in Table 4.2, there are five paths from Start to End in this graph, and the longest path has a project duration of 18. Therefore, the critical path is denoted by Start–B–C–D–End with critical activities B, C, and D. The forward pass of the CPM algorithm assumes that both activities A and B start at time 0. The ES of activity C depends on the completion of activities A and B. Since activity B is the longer of the two activities, activity C cannot begin until activity B is completed, which is at time period 7. Activity D has only one predecessor — activity C — and can begin as early as

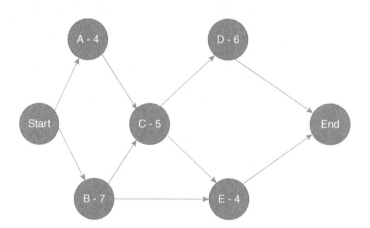

Fig. 4.3. CPM example

Table 4.2. Network paths and lengths

Path	Activities	Expected Duration (Weeks)
1	Start–B–C–D–End	18
2	Start–B–C–E–End	16
3	Start–A–C–D–End	15
4	Start–A–C–E–End	13
5	Start–B–E–End	11

activity C is completed, time period 12. Activity E must wait for both activities B and C to be completed before it may begin. Although activity B may be completed by time period 7, the ES of activity E is 12, since it must wait for activity C to finish. The End milestone is reached when both activities D and E are completed. In this case, activity D cannot finish before 18, while activity E can finish by 16. Therefore, $EF_{END} = 18$.

Once the End node is reached by the forward pass of the algorithm, the project duration and LF_{END} are known; in this case, they are equal to 18. The backward pass calculates LS and LF for each activity. For example, LF is 18 for both tasks D and E, implying that LS is 12 for activity D (its duration is 6), and LS is 14 for activity E (its duration is 4). If we consider activity C, its LF is the minimum of 12 and 14 since its two successor activities are D and E. Once activity C's LF is established to be 12, its LS is calculated as $12 - 5 = 7$, where 5 is C's duration time. The backward pass continues in this fashion until the Start node is reached. A full set of results from the CPM algorithm for this example is given in Table 4.3.

In this example, activities B, C, and D were all critical, as they lay on the critical path. If the duration times of any of these three activities were to increase by, say, 1, then the duration of the project would also increase by 1. A project manager must carefully monitor critical activities, as delays in their completion impact the overall project's completion date. In Table 4.3, each critical activity has the following property: LF − ES = duration time. In general, we refer to the *slack* or *total slack* of activity *j* by

Table 4.3. CPM calculations

Activity	Duration	Earliest Start Time	Earliest Finish Time	Latest Start Time	Latest Finish Time
Start	0	0	0	0	0
A	4	0	4	3	7
B	7	0	7	0	7
C	5	7	12	7	12
D	6	12	18	12	18
E	4	12	16	14	18
End	0	18	18	18	18

the formula: $LFj - ESj - tj$, where tj is the duration of activity j. An activity is a critical activity if and only if its slack is 0. Non-critical activities will have slack >0. These activities offer a project manager more flexibility *vis-à-vis* scheduling them, as they may be delayed — up to a point — without impacting a project's duration. In our example, activity A has a slack of 3, and activity E has a slack of 2. Activity A, for example, may be started as early as 0 and may be finished as late as 7. Since its duration time is 4, $7 - 0 - 4 = 3$. Although there are other definitions of slack, the definition used here is most common in project management software and most commonly used in practice.

2. Introducing Uncertainty into Scheduling

A key assumption in using CPM and Gantt charts is that activity duration times are deterministic. In certain projects, high levels of uncertainty regarding activity duration times may exist. Moreover, due to the non-repetitive nature of projects, limited information on actual duration times may exist for certain activities. When the probabilistic nature of duration times must be explicitly modeled, an alternative solution approach is needed for scheduling activities. PERT — Program Evaluation and Review Technique — was developed to support project scheduling when task duration times are assumed to be stochastic.

PERT assumes that managers can estimate three points related to an activity's duration time: (i) most optimistic duration time, denoted by a_i for activity i; (ii) most pessimistic duration time, denoted by b_i for activity i; and (iii) most likely duration time, denoted by m_i for activity i. Using these three-point estimates, the mean μ and variance σ^2 (or standard deviation σ) may be estimated for each activity by the formulas:

$$\mu_i = (a_i + b_i + (4*m_i))/6$$

and

$$\sigma_i^2 = (b_i - a_i)^2/36.$$

PERT assumes that activity durations in a project network are statistically independent random variables that follow a beta distribution.

In practice, this assumption is questionable. If a resource is assigned to multiple activities in a project and if that resource is an efficient resource, all of the activities assigned to that resource may finish ahead of schedule. The duration times of the activities assigned to this particular resource are not truly independent, as they all involve the same, efficient resource.

If we continue to assume that activity duration times are independent, then the expected duration time of any path in a project network graph can be found by summing the expected duration times of all of the activities on the path. Likewise, the variances of the duration times of activities along a path may be summed to compute the variance associated with the path (the standard deviation of the path duration time is the square root of the variance of the path duration time). From the *Central Limit Theorem* in statistics, the distribution of the sum of independent random variables is approximately normally distributed. We can use the normal distribution theory to compute the probability of completing a project by some threshold due date t as follows:

$$P(X \leq \tau) = P,$$

where X is the expected project duration and Z is the standard normal distribution with mean 0 and variance 1.

Consider the example of the project network depicted above in Fig. 4.3. This example can be extended to illustrate PERT by assuming that the duration times for the activities are stochastic. It is assumed that activity duration times can be estimated by their optimistic, pessimistic, and most likely values, as shown in Table 4.4.

Table 4.4.   Data for PERT example

Task	Predecessors	Optimistic	Pessimistic	Most Likely	Expected Duration	Variance
A		3	4	6	4.17	0.25
B		2	7	10	6.67	1.78
C	A, B	4	5	12	6.00	1.78
D	C	5	6	7	6.00	0.11
E	B, C,	1	4	20	6.33	9.00

In this network, there are five paths from Start to End, as shown in Table 4.5.

Of these, B–C–E is the longest path with an expected project duration of 19. The variance associated with this path is 12.6. If senior management is interested in the probability that the project will be completed by time period 24, the project manager can use the calculation, $Z = (24-19) / \sqrt{12.6} = 1.41$. Using a standard normal distribution table, we find that a Z-score of 1.41 corresponds to a probability of 0.921. Therefore, a project manager, based on a PERT analysis, can inform senior management that the project has a 92.1% probability of finishing by the desired due date 24.

The major shortcoming of the PERT method is that it ignores other paths in the network that, due to variability and "bad luck", may become the critical path in certain instances. If a non-critical path, in fact, becomes critical due to an unexpected delay in a non-critical activity, then the PERT estimate of a project's completion time is optimistic. A project manager may unintentionally raise stakeholders' expectations if the project manager solely employs the PERT method to estimate project completion time.

In dealing with uncertainty in duration times, PERT offers a project manager a tool that calculates the project's duration using straightforward (closed-form) formulas. However, for some projects, the shortcoming of the PERT method — being overly optimistic in estimating project duration — results in a Monte Carlo simulation model being developed in order to estimate project duration. In a simulation model, random

Table 4.5. Paths from Start to End in the PERT example

Path	Expected Duration	Variance
A–C–E	16.5	11.0
A–C–D	16.2	2.1
B–C–D	18.7	3.7
B–C–E	19.0	12.6
B–E	13.0	10.8

duration times for each task are generated, assuming some underlying distribution (often, in practice, it is assumed that duration times follow a beta distribution). In each run of the simulation, random duration times are generated for each task, and the CPM algorithm is run in order to compute the critical path and project duration for that instance (or realization) of task duration times. By running the simulation for multiple instances, a project manager can construct a frequency distribution or histogram of project duration and determine the probabilities for each task that, in fact, will show it to be a critical task. In addition to providing a point estimate of project duration, a simulation model, typically, provides confidence intervals around the point estimate, providing a project manager with a statistically robust range of expected outcomes. The Criticality Index (CI) of a particular task is the percentage of simulation runs in which that task fell on the critical path. Although simulation — compared with PERT — will provide more accurate estimates of project completion times and the likelihood of a particular task being critical, most commercial project management software packages do not include a simulation capability.

Goldratt's Critical Chain method is another alternative for dealing with uncertainty in task duration times. The method is based on Goldratt's Theory of Constraints, applied to project management. The fundamental idea of the method is to focus on overall project completion time and critical (bottleneck) tasks. Goldratt defines the concept of a project buffer. In essence, a project manager keeps a reserve of time in the project plan, similar to how a reserve of cash may be used to cover unexpected budget shortfalls. For example, if the expected completion time based on, say, CPM, is T, then a project manager will add a buffer b to this value and plan for a project completion time of $T + b$.

Conceptually, the buffer is placed at the end of a project, immediately preceding the End node. Since each activity's duration time is random, having a pooled buffer — rather than a buffer associated with each task — allows a project manager to pool risks and variability associated with all activities simultaneously. For example, consider two activities, A and B. Each activity is normally distributed. Activity A has a mean of 20 and a variance of 25, and activity B has a mean of 30 and a variance of 64. If a 95% probability of being completed on time is desired, then, based on a Z-score of 1.64, 28.2 and 43.1 time periods need to be allowed for A and B, respectively. By comparison, if A and B are pooled (essentially treating two activities as a single activity), the pooled activity is also normally distributed with a mean of 50 and a variance of 89. In this case, a 95% completion probability corresponds to 65.5 time periods. The pooled approach enabled a project manager to shave 5.8 time periods from the stated completion time and maintain a 95% probability of completing the project on time.

One shortcoming of Goldratt's method is that calculation of the required project buffer is somewhat arbitrary. One formula is proposed by Newbold (1998) as follows:

$$(\Sigma_{\text{tasks } j \text{ on the critical path}} (b_j - \mu_j)^2))^{0.5}.$$

By adding a schedule buffer to the CPM estimate of project duration, a project manager arrives at a more realistic estimate of the overall project completion time. A project buffer provides a reserve in the project schedule to enable it to tolerate delays in certain activities and yet maintain on-time delivery of key milestones.

Goldratt's method, however, has not been widely adopted by the project management community. Its methodology is perceived as being theoretical and belonging to Goldratt's Theory of Constraints, which has been more applicable to production scheduling rather than project scheduling. Moreover, project management software does not, in general, include Goldratt's methodology, making it less accessible to the practitioner community.

4.2. Scheduling in the PTB

Once a scenario is opened, a user can begin to plan the project. The "Plan Execute Control" menu tab is presented in Fig. 4.4.

Fig. 4.4.   Plan Execute Control menu tab

4.2.1. *The Plan menu group*

Under the "Plan Execute Control" menu tab is the "Plan" menu group including the following buttons:

- **Plan Default** — Sets all unplanned tasks to the earliest possible start time and, in case of tasks with multiple modes (alternative ways to perform the task), selects the mode with the least expected cost. This cost is calculated according to Mode Fixed Cost and required resource cost. This mode is also typically the one with the longest duration.
- **Plan Early** — This is used to schedule all planned tasks to the early start time without changing the current mode of the task.
- **The Gantt Chart** — Shows the planned schedule of the project. In the Gantt view, it is possible to click on any task icon to view the planning screen for that task. It is also possible to change the task start time by dragging its bar on the Gantt chart to the required start time.

4.2.2. *Task planning*

The first step before running the simulation is to plan the project tasks by setting a start time and choosing the mode of operation for each task. Task Planning starts by double-clicking on the task bar in the Gantt chart or by clicking on the task node in the network view.

If multiple modes are available to carry out a particular task, the user has to select a preferred mode of operation. Each mode of operation specifies the duration of the task, the amount of resources necessary, the cost, and, if applicable, the quality parameters used to calculate the benefits of the system. The PTB tool enables a user to quickly do "what-if" sensitivity analysis by trying different combinations of modes for different tasks associated with multiple modes. The PTB can quickly provide feedback on the benefits and pitfalls of different mode combinations.

Setting a Default Plan — A default plan can be implemented using the Plan Default button (as shown above in Fig. 4.4) in the Plan and Execute menu. The start period of each task in the default plan (early start) is automatically calculated according to the duration and predecessors of the individual tasks. The automatically calculated planned start period is the first period that the task can be started. The user may alter this time as explained later.

When the Plan Default button is pressed, the tasks in the network change color, as they are all planned (see Figs. 4.4 and 4.5).

Planning of Specific Tasks — Specific task planning (one task at a time) is performed through the network view or the Gantt view. A double-click on a task node in the network or on the task bar in the Gantt chart opens the task planning window (see Fig. 4.6).

The task-planning window presents the following information:

- **Task Name**
- **Income** — The amount of cash generated at the end of the task.

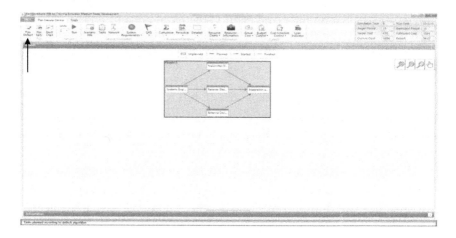

Fig. 4.5. Tasks planned by plan default

Fig. 4.6. Task planning view

- **Cost of Split** — The cost of each split (break) in the task execution (if splitting is enabled).
- **Description** — A short textual description of the task.
- **Actual Start** — The time at which the task started in the current simulation run, if applicable.
- **Actual Finish** — The time at which the task finished in the current simulation run, if applicable.
  - The actual start time is displayed only after the task starts.
  - The actual finish time is displayed only after the task ends.
- **Current Status** — The current status of the task (unplanned, planned, started, finished).
- **Mode** — The mode (that is, a team of resources that may feasibly execute a task with associated duration times, costs, and quality parameters) currently selected for a planned task.

Choosing an Execution Mode for a Task — The task execution mode is set in the task planning window. A table at the bottom of this view lists the available modes for that task. Choosing a mode sets the following parameters that are displayed in the table:

- **Optimistic Duration, Most Likely Duration, Pessimistic Duration** — For each mode, a user inputs parameters to estimate the "actual" execution time of every task (randomly generated from a triangle distribution). In deterministic scenarios, the three parameters are set equal to each other.
- **Fixed Cost** — The one-time cost necessary to perform the task in the selected mode. This cost does not depend on the task duration and the resources used to perform the task.
- **Resources Needed** — The number of resource units of each resource type required to perform the task in the relevant mode.
- **The Start Time of the Task** is entered at the **Start At** field and needs to be followed by clicking on the **Apply Start Time** button.
- **The Change Status** — This button is used to change a task from the "unplanned" to the "planned" status.
- **Task Splitting** — In some scenarios, it is possible to split a task during its execution. Splitting a task involves stopping the task at a certain

period before it is completed, and restarting it again on a later time period. Splitting a task is performed by setting two parameters:

○ **Split at (Split Start Time)** — The time in which a split (break) in the task is planned.

○ **Restart at (Split Stop Time)** — The time in which the split (break) in the task is finished and task processing resumes.

After setting the two parameters, click on the "Apply Split" button to activate the split. It might be necessary to split some tasks. This is the case when the availability of resources is stochastic (for example due to absenteeism or machine breakdown) and when a task that started cannot be continued due to a lack of resources. In such cases, it may be necessary to split the task.

In the Gantt view, it is possible to see if certain tasks overlap in the schedule. If an overlap is unwanted, for example, due to the lack of resources, it is possible to change the start period or to split tasks.

4.3. Monte Carlo Simulation

Monte Carlo methods use repeated random sampling to obtain numerical results. The PTB includes a Monte Carlo simulation feature. The Monte Carlo method allows the user to perform quantitative risk analysis. If the project model includes uncertain task durations, a project manager can obtain estimates regarding the likelihood of completing the project by a specific time period, at a specific cost, with the probability that a specific task will be critical.

This feature is enabled once a user creates a project plan. To access the simulation feature, a user may click on the Analyze button in the Monte Carlo buttons group under the Tools menu (Fig. 4.7).

After clicking on the Analyze button, the Monte Carlo Simulation view appears (Fig. 4.8).

Fig. 4.7.   Monte Carlo button

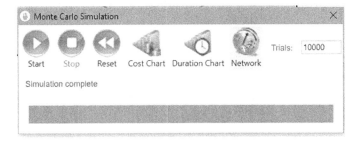

Fig. 4.8. Monte Carlo Simulation view

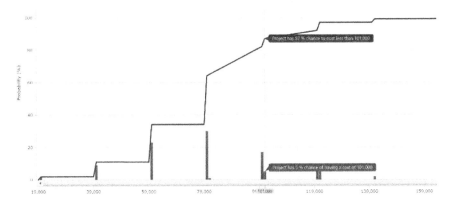

Fig. 4.9. Cost Chart view

To run the simulation, enter the number of Trials, that is, the number of times that the PTB will automatically run the project, and click on the Start button. Once the simulation is finished, three views are available — the Cost Chart view for the project cost distribution, the Duration Chart view for the project finish time distribution, and the Network view for the critical task information.

The Project Finish Time chart can be viewed by clicking on the Duration Chart button. This view (Fig. 4.10) shows the probability that the project will finish **in** a specific time period (the chart bars) and the probability that the project will finish **by** a specific time period (the blue line). To view the exact numbers, a user moves the mouse cursor over the relevant chart part (the bars or the line).

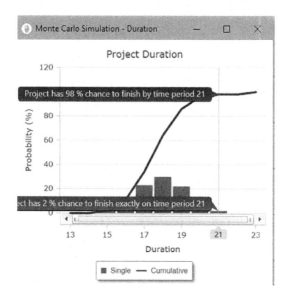

Fig. 4.10. Monte Carlo Project finish time view

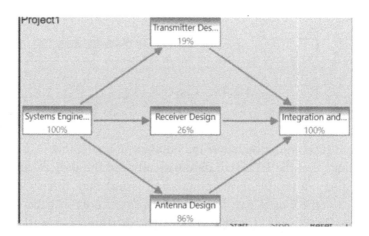

Fig. 4.11. Critical Task network view

The Critical Task network view is available by clicking on the Network button. This view (Fig. 4.11) shows the probability that each task will be critical.

4.4. Summary

Project scheduling is widely used as part of project management. Gantt charts are common communication tools that help project teams coordinate their effort by specifying what needs to be done and when. More sophisticated tools like the CPM are the backbone of most project management software. Gantt charts, critical path analysis, and Monte Carlo simulation are all built into the PTB and can be easily accessed. A project manager can use these tools effectively and efficiently to support the project scheduling decision-making process. Typically, a project manager will iterate between proposing certain scheduling parameters, testing them in a particular PTB scenario, and then refining them.

Chapter 5

Resource Management

5.1. Allocating Resources and Selecting Modes

Project activities are performed by a variety of resources. Human resources, like engineers or technicians, are the backbone of high tech projects, while equipment, like bulldozers, cranes, and heavy trucks, are used along with human resources in many construction projects. Resource allocation is an important part of project management. Resource allocation is a multi-level process. At the highest level, resources are allocated to a project on either a dedicated full-time or a part-time, as-needed basis. At the next level, resources are allocated to activities. The type and quantity of resources allocated to perform an activity determine the duration of the activity, its cost, its quality, and the resulting deliverables. In many projects, some activities have more than one resource combination that can perform the activity. For example, it is possible to dig a tunnel with one bulldozer and a single operator, working eight or 10 hours a day. It is also possible to perform the same activity with a single bulldozer and three operators working three 8-hour shifts. Other options may be considered, for example, to assign two bulldozers and two operators or two bulldozers and six operators, etc. Each of these possibilities is called a **mode** of operation (in short, mode). The selection of a mode (or combination of resources) for an activity is a decision that influences the duration of the activity, its cost, its quality, and the risks involved. Depending on the criticality of the activity, mode choice may also influence the overall project, including its schedule, its budget, and the quality of deliverables. A project manager must take into account the possible modes, the availability of resources, and the resulting duration, cost, risk, and quality of the activity in order to select the preferred mode.

The decisions of allocating resources to a project team and to individual project activities are interdependent. A resource can be allocated full time to a project for its entire duration or, alternatively, it may be assigned to a project on a temporary basis when needed. Resources allocated full time to a single project are called *renewable resources* as their availability is "renewed" each period. In other words, if a person is assigned full time to a project, the project manager has full control of that resource across the project's entire time horizon. A project manager has to assign an adequate workload to each renewable resource, as otherwise these resources might be idle even though their cost or salary is still charged to the project. Another option is to employ resources only when needed and to pay only for the actual time the resource is used on the project. Such resources are known as *depleting resources*. In many projects, the total availability of depleting resources is limited. The available time (or budget) of a depleting resource is consumed when the resource is used to perform the project activities. An example is an expert consultant who is available to work 100 hours on the project. As the consultant is used on the project, the remaining number of available hours is reduced.

The advantage of renewable resources is that a project manager has full control and complete authority regarding resource utilization. The disadvantage of renewable resources is the cost of idle time that is charged to the project when the resource is not engaged on a project task. To avoid idle time, a resource leveling strategy may be adopted — an effort to schedule the project so that the same number of renewable resources of each type is required in each time period and to assign this number of renewable resources of each type to the project.

We present examples of heuristic algorithms that may be used to solve the two classic scheduling problems associated with resource management that typically confront a project manager: (i) the resource leveling problem and (ii) the resource allocation problem. The resource leveling problem involves scheduling non-critical activities in a project. Critical activities are assumed to be fixed with respect to earliest start dates and latest finish dates. However, non-critical activities may be shifted in the project schedule so that they start and/or finish during time periods coinciding with non-peak demand for a critical, limited resource. By shifting non-critical activities in the project schedule, a project manager can smooth out demand for the critical, limited resource, thereby minimizing the maximum number of resources that would be needed in each period over the project's life cycle.

The resource leveling problem belongs to a class of combinatorial optimization problems that are NP-complete and is, therefore, solved by a heuristic algorithm. One such solution approach is presented using the example described in Table 5.1.

The resource leveling heuristic algorithm first finds the unconstrained critical path assuming that no resource requirements were stated. In this case, the unconstrained critical path is A–C–D–G, with a project duration of 18. The critical activities A, C, D, and G must start at times 0, 5, 11, and 14 in order for the project to be completed by time 18. These activities, with respect to scheduling decisions, can be "removed" from the resource leveling problem since the project manager cannot delay any of these activities without delaying the overall project. The resource leveling problem, therefore, focuses on scheduling the non-critical activities, B, E, and F in this example.

The heuristic algorithm's initial step is to assume that each of the non-critical activities begins at its earliest possible start time, that is, activity B would start at time 0, activity E would start at time 11, and activity F would start at time 14. Table 5.2 presents a profile of resource usage, period-by-period, over the project horizon, assuming that non-critical activities started at their earliest possible start times.

Table 5.1. Project data for resource levelling example

Activity	Duration	Req. Resource	Total Resource	Predecessors	Early Start	Slack
A	5	8	40		0	0
B	4	5	20		0	7
C	6	6	36	A	5	0
D	3	8	24	B, C	11	0
E	5	3	30	C	11	2
F	2	4	8	D	14	2
G	4	4	16	D	14	0

Table 5.2.   Resource leveling example: Initial step of the heuristic

Week	A	B	C	D	E	F	G	Total
1	8	5						13
2	8	5						13
3	8	5						13
4	8	5						13
5	8							8
6			6					6
7			6					6
8			6					6
9			6					6
10			6					6
11			6					6
12				8	3			11
13				8	3			11
14				8	3			11
15					3	4	4	11
16					3	4	4	11
17							4	4
18							4	4

In the initial schedule, a peak demand of 13 resource units is encountered in periods 1–4. Under this scheme, a project manager would be required to hire or purchase 13 units of the resource or risk delaying the project. The initial schedule's usage of the resource is not very smooth. After peaking at 13 in periods 1–4, 8 units of the resource are required in period 5, and 6 units are required in periods 6–11. However, in period 12, resource usage once again spikes back up to 11, before tailing off at the conclusion of the project.

Is it possible to dampen the peak resource usage? The heuristic ranks the non-critical activities in non-ascending order of slack: B, E, F (ties are broken arbitrarily). The heuristic considers shifting the start of activity B by 7 time periods so that its available slack is depleted — see Table 5.3.

Table 5.3. Shift of start time of non-critical task B

Week	A	B	C	D	E	F	G	Total
1	8							8
2	8							8
3	8							8
4	8							8
5	8							8
6			6					6
7			6					6
8		5	6					11
9		5	6					11
10		5	6					11
11		5	6					11
12				8	3			11
13				8	3			11
14				8	3			11
15					3	4	4	11
16					3	4	4	11
17							4	4
18							4	4

In considering the updated resource usage profile, the peak demand for the resource decreased from 13 in Table 5.2 to 11 in Table 5.3. This was accomplished by shifting the start time of activity B from its earliest start time — 1 — to its latest start time — 8. In the updated schedule depicted in Table 5.3, only activities E and F have slack >0. However, a further reduction in the peak resource requirement cannot be attained by shifting the start time of either activity E or activity F.

The resource allocation problem, with renewable resources, is the most popular resource scheduling problem encountered by project managers. The objective is to assign a fixed supply of resources to activities and schedule those activities so that project duration is minimized. Unlike the resource leveling problem, which assumes that project duration is fixed, the resource allocation problem allows project duration to vary. The most common form of the resource allocation problem with renewable resources also belongs to the NP-complete class of combinatorial optimization problems and is typically solved by heuristic algorithms in practice.

Many of the heuristic algorithms for the resource allocation problem begin by finding the unconstrained critical path. The heuristic approaches examine the unconstrained critical path solution and detect any time periods in which required resource usage is infeasible (due to the lack of available resources). For an infeasible time period, the activities that require the scarce resource are prioritized according to different heuristic rules. The scarce resource is then allocated to the competing activities in priority order, which may result in a delay in the overall project completion time. The heuristics strive to minimize such delays. However, project delays may be inevitable in practice since the supply of available resources is assumed to be fixed for the duration of the project. (In practice, a delay that exceeds a stakeholder-imposed threshold could result in additional funding for the project to invest in increasing the supply and availability of scarce resources.)

We will illustrate four of the common heuristic solution approaches for the resource allocation problem. The longest duration first heuristic chooses a feasible (with respect to precedence constraints) activity with the longest duration time at each step of the algorithm. Note that this algorithm does not use an activity's resource requirement in selecting and prioritizing a particular activity. The solution approach is demonstrated using the project data described in Table 5.4.

Table 5.4. Data for the longest duration first heuristic example

Activity	Predecessor	Duration	Resource Requirement
A	—	2	3
B	—	8	5
C	—	4	4
D	A	3	2
E	C	5	4
F	B, D, E	6	2

In this example, assume that 10 units of a single, scarce resource are available for the project. The activities are ordered in non-ascending order of duration time: {B, F, E, C, D, A}. The unconstrained critical path is C–E–F, resulting in a project completion time of 15. The heuristic starts at time 0 and lists the activities — A, B, C — that may be started at that time, based on precedence constraints. Since these three activities, together, require 12 units of resource, they may not all be started at time 0. Based on the ordering of activities, B and C — since they have the longest duration times, relative to activity A — are started at time 0. Activity C finishes at time period 4. At that point, the heuristic once again lists all of the activities that may be started at the time — A and E. Since the duration time of activity E exceeds the duration time of activity A, activity E is selected by the algorithm to start at period 4. At time period 8, activity B is completed. At that point, the list of activities that may be feasibly started includes activity A only. Therefore, activity A is started at time 8. When activity E is completed at time period 9, there are no activities that may be feasibly started (activity D can only be started when activity A is completed). Activity A is completed in time period 10, and activity D may be started at that time. Finally, activity F can be started when activity D is completed in period 13. The overall project is completed in period 19 (in contrast with the unconstrained critical path solution of 15). The schedule of activities for the project is summarized in Table 5.5.

Table 5.5. Solution to the example project using the longest duration first heuristic

Activity	Unconstrained Start Time	Resource-Constrained Start Time
A	0	8
B	0	0
C	0	0
D	2	10
E	4	4
F	9	13

The ACTIM and ACTRES heuristics are two popular solution approaches to the resource allocation problem. At each step of the algorithm, ACTIM prioritizes an activity such that the path from that activity to the end of the project is longest. Similarly, at each iteration of the ACTRES algorithm, the heuristic chooses an activity such that the "weighted path" from that activity to the end of the project is longest where the "weighted path" is defined by the sum of the products of each activity's duration time and resource requirement along the path. Both heuristics are illustrated with the data in Table 5.6.

In this example, assume that 7 units of a scarce resource are available. The ACTIM heuristic initially finds the unconstrained critical path. In this example, the path A–D is the critical path with a project completion time of 10. Each activity's latest start time (according to the critical path method solution) is required as input for the ACTIM heuristic. Each activity is then given a "score" or rating based on the difference between the unconstrained critical path project duration and the activity's latest start time. The ACTIM scores for the example are given in Table 5.7.

The activities are ordered in non-ascending order of ACTIM score — {A, B, D, E, C}. At time period 0, the activities — A, B, C — may be feasibly started, if a scarce resource was not present. However, the scarce resource limits a project manager's flexibility with respect to scheduling. Using the ACTIM heuristic, activities A and B are selected initially at time period 0. At time period 2, activity A is completed, and activity D may be started. Likewise, at time period 3, activity B is completed, and activity E may be started. When activity E is completed in time period 9, activity C

Table 5.6. Example of project data to illustrate ACTIM and ACTRES heuristics

Activity	Predecessor	Duration	Resource Requirement
A	—	2	2
B	—	3	1
C	—	5	6
D	A	8	3
E	B	6	3

Table 5.7. ACTIM scores for the example

Activity	Latest Start Time	ACTIM Score
A	0	10
B	1	9
C	5	5
D	2	8
E	4	6

cannot be started. Activity C requires 6 units of resource, and activity D, which is ongoing in period 9, employs 3 units of resource (7 units of resource are available to the project). Therefore, activity C must wait for activity D to complete in time period 10. The overall project is completed in time period 15. Due to the relative high resource requirement of activity C, the project is delayed by 5 time periods, compared with the unconstrained critical path solution.

In the ACTRES heuristic, each activity's score is computed by the following procedure:

Step 1: For each activity j, compute the product c_j of its duration time and resource requirement

Step 2: Find the longest path from activity j to the terminal node of the project network; let S_j denote the set of activities (nodes) associated with this path

Step 3: Let the ACTRES score = $\sum c_i$ over all activities $i \varepsilon S_j$.

In our example, the ACTRES scores for activities C, D, and E are 30, 24, and 18, respectively. For activity A, the ACTRES score is 4 + 24 (the ACTRES score of D) or 28. Likewise, the ACTRES score for activity B is 21 = 3 + 18 (the ACTRES score of activity E).

The algorithm sorts the activities in non-ascending order of ACTRES score — {C, A, D, B, E}. At the outset of the project's time horizon, activities A, B, and C are candidate activities to be started. Activity C has the highest priority, based on its ACTRES score. Although activity A has a greater ACTRES score than activity B, activity A cannot be started at time 0 since insufficient resources are available (having been allocated to activity C). Therefore, activity B, which has a resource requirement of 1 unit, is bumped up in the schedule and started at time period 0 along with activity C. As long as activity C is ongoing, no other activity may be started. When activity C is completed in time period 5, activity A can be started. Since activity B has also terminated at that point, activity E can also be started at time period 5. Activity D has activity A as a predecessor activity and can only be started at time period 7 when activity A is completed. The overall project, therefore, is completed by time period 15.

In comparing the resource-constrained solution, calculated by the ACTRES heuristic, with the unconstrained critical path, we see that both A and D — which formed the critical activities in the unconstrained solution — were each delayed by 5 time periods, respectively. The source of the delay was that activity C — with its very high ACTRES score (due to its high resource requirement) — had priority and "starved" all of the other activities (except activity B) from sharing in the resource while it was active.

A comparison of the ACTIM and ACTRES solutions is given in Table 5.8.

Although both heuristics found an identical project duration — 15, in larger problems — this condition is not guaranteed to hold. The problem data will determine which heuristic yields a more efficient solution. In general, the choice of which heuristic to deploy may be based on the importance of weighing resource requirements in prioritizing a project's activities. Even in the relatively small project network considered in this example, the sequence in which the activities were performed differed

Table 5.8.   Comparison of ACTIM and ACTRES solutions for the example

Activity	ACTIM Start Time	ACTRES Start Time
A	0	5
B	0	0
C	10	0
D	2	7
E	3	5

widely. In practice, there may be some unstated business conditions that favor one schedule over another.

The last heuristic algorithm that we will illustrate for resource allocation is known as the Minimum Total Slack Time heuristic. Conceptually, at any time period where the demand for a scarce resource exceeds supply, the algorithm prioritizes the contending activities based on total slack. Activities with higher values of total slack can be delayed, since a delay in such an activity may tend to minimize the impact on the overall project completion time.

The description of the heuristic is presented via an example. Consider the project whose data is presented in Table 5.9.

Table 5.10 depicts the resource usage pattern associated with the unconstrained critical path solution for the project presented in Table 5.9. Assume that 3 units of resource are available for the project.

The solution in Table 5.10 is not feasible since the demand for resources in time periods 3 and 4 exceed the supply. The project cannot execute activities B, C, and D simultaneously. The heuristic computes the slack associated with each of the three competing activities. Activity B is on the critical path (A–B–F–G), and its slack is 0. Non-critical activities C and D have a slack of 6 and 2, respectively. Since activity B has the minimum slack, it has the highest priority with respect to being assigned a resource. Since activity B only requires 2 of the 3 resource units, sufficient

Table 5.9. Example project to illustrate the minimum total slack time heuristic

Activity	Predecessors	Resource Required	Duration
A	—	2	2
B	A	2	4
C	A	2	2
D	A	1	6
E	B	2	2
F	B	1	4
G	C, D, E, F	2	3

Table 5.10.   Resource usage for the unconstrained critical path solution

Activity						Period							
	1	2	3	4	5	6	7	8	9	10	11	12	13
A	2	2											
B			2	2	2	2							
C			2	2									
D			1	1	1	1	1	1					
E							2	2					
F							1	1	1	1			
G											2	2	2
Resource	2	2	5	5	3	3	4	4	1	1	2	2	2

Table 5.11.   Activity C is delayed

Activity						Period							
	1	2	3	4	5	6	7	8	9	10	11	12	13
A	2	2											
B			2	2	2	2							
C							2	2					
D			1	1	1	1	1	1					
E							2	2					
F							1	1	1	1			
G											2	2	2
Resource	2	2	3	3	3	3	6	6	1	1	2	2	2

resource capacity exists to start activities B and D in time period 3. Activity C, however, is delayed, as depicted in Table 5.11.

Once activity B is complete, two units of resource are released. Conceivably, activity C could be started at that point. In this example, as shown in Table 5.11, four activities are competing for the resource in time period 7. Together, their resource requirements sum to 6, implying an infeasible condition. Since activity D is ongoing, it is allowed to

Table 5.12. Activities C and E are delayed

Activity	1	2	3	4	5	6	7	8	9	10	11	12	13
						Period							
A	2	2											
B			2	2	2	2							
C									2	2			
D			1	1	1	1	1	1					
E									2	2			
F							1	1	1	1			
G											2	2	2
Resource	2	2	3	3	3	3	2	2	5	5	2	2	2

complete, thereby leaving activities C, E, and F to compete for two resource units. Slack is recompeted for these three activities as follows: C – 2, E – 2, F – 0. Since activity F is on the critical path, it is given top priority. Since one resource unit is dedicated to activity D and since one other resource unit is allocated to activity F, only one unit of resource is left over. Since activities C and E each require two units of resources, they cannot be feasibly started at time period 7. Therefore, the third and final resource unit available is left idle. Activities C and E are delayed, as depicted in Table 5.12.

By delaying activities C and E by two time periods, the demand for resources in period 9 exceeds supply. Activities C and E are competing for two available resource units (it is assumed that activity F which is ongoing in period 9 will not be interrupted). At this point, a delay in the start time of either activity C or E will result in a delay in the completion of the overall project, as both activities have 0 slack remaining. Since both activities have identical slack, identical durations, and identical resource requirements, it is arbitrary as to which activity is delayed. As shown in Table 5.13, we chose to delay activity E, thereby delaying the overall project by two time periods.

A research team at the Katholieke Universiteit Leuven (Belgium) developed an educational project scheduling software called RESCON

Table 5.13. Feasible solution obtained by the minimum total slack time heuristic

	Period														
Activity	1	2	3	4	5	6	7	8	9	10	11	12	13	14	15
A	2	2													
B			2	2	2	2									
C									2	2					
D			1	1	1	1	1	1							
E											2	2			
F							1	1	1	1					
G													2	2	2
Resource	2	2	3	3	3	3	2	2	3	3	2	2	2	2	2

(from RESource CONstrained). RESCON solves the resource-constrained project scheduling problem for the case of a single mode and deterministic resource availability, using several scheduling algorithms that are embedded in the software. More information about RESCON is available at http://feb.kuleuven.be/rescon/. RESCON is available free of charge.

5.2. Resource Management in the PTB Resource Information

Resource information is presented in the lower part of the screen by pressing the Resource Information button under the Resource Information menu group in the "Plan Execute Control" menu tab (see Fig. 5.1).

The resource information is summarized in a table that includes the following data:

- **Name** — the name of the resource type.
- **Available Units** — the available quantity of the resource at the current time.
- **Units Available in Lead Time** — the quantity of the resource that will be available after the assign-and-release lead time elapses.
- **Cost per Period** — per period cost of the resource while the resource is performing a task.

Name	Available Units	Units Available in Lead Time	Cost/Period	Idle Cost/Period	Releasing Cost	Assigning Cost	Show Up Probability (%)	Releasing Lead Time	Assigning Lead Time	Minimum Units	Maximum
Engineers	20	20	100	50	50	50	80	1	1	1	30
Technicians	20	20	50	10	40	20	85	1	1	2	50

Fig. 5.1. Resource information

- **Idle cost per Period** — per period cost of the resource while not performing a task.
- **Releasing Cost** — the cost of reducing resource's availability by one unit.
- **Assigning Cost** — the cost of increasing a resource's availability by one unit.
- **Show up Probability (%)** — the probability that a resource unit will be available to work on the project's tasks in any given period (displayed in percentage). If, for example, the Show up Probability is 95%, then there is a 5% chance, for every resource unit of this type, of not showing up for a specific time period.
- **Releasing Lead Time** — the number of time periods required to release a resource unit.
- **Assigning Lead Time** — the number of time periods required to assign a resource unit.
- **Minimum Units** — the minimum number of resource units the user can use.
- **Maximum Units** — the maximum number of resource units the user can use.

Some resource information and financial information is available only after the project tasks are planned, i.e., a mode is selected and a starting time is assigned.

5.3. Resource Usage

By pressing the Resource Charts button under the Resource Information menu group in the "Plan Execute Control" menu tab, it is possible to present a resource usage chart in the upper part of the screen for each resource type, see Fig. 5.2.

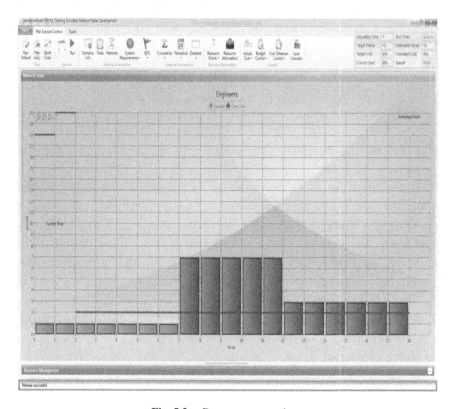

Fig. 5.2.   Resource usage chart

This chart displays the amount of resources required of this resource type for each period. It is possible to see the expected available amount as a blue line. A red bar indicates a period in which demand for the resource exceeds available supply. A green bar represents a period with sufficient resources.

The current time period is depicted by a vertical line. All information to the left of the line shows what actually happened in the project. Information to the right of the line shows what is expected to happen.

To view tasks requiring the resource type in a specific period, click on the bar of that period to open the resource usage details for that period, see Fig. 5.3.

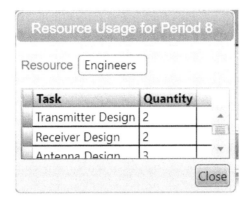

Fig. 5.3. Resource usage for a specific period

If a project schedule is not feasible due to a resource constraint being violated, the user can perform any of the following remedial steps:

1. Choose a mode of execution which requires less units of that resource type, for the tasks that did not start yet, and use the resource unit in the violated period.
2. Assign more units of this type.
3. Change the start time of the tasks that did not start yet and use this resource type.
4. Split an activity that has already started.

5.4. Assigning and Releasing Resources

In some scenarios, it is possible to change the level of certain resources within preset minimum and maximum levels in order to reach optimal performance. There is an assigning-and-releasing lead time for each resource type. This is the time it takes to assign or release a unit of the resource once a decision is made and entered in the manage resource screen, as shown in Fig. 5.1. This window displays relevant information and allows assigning or releasing resources.

To assign or release units of a resource, select the desired resource type by clicking on the "Select Resource" button in the resource management screen. The cost of assigning or releasing a resource is found in the manage resources screen. While there may be a cost for changing the amount of resource units, it might be advantageous relative to a project's overall cost.

5.5. Summary

Project activities are performed by a variety of resources. Selection of resources, their allocation to project activities, and resource usage planning are major tasks of the project manager. Tools for resource allocation and resource leveling are essential for the development of a good project plan and its execution. Project success is dependent on proper management of resources throughout a project's life cycle.

Chapter 6

Budgeting

6.1. The Project Cost Structure

Projects are like cars running on fuel. There should be enough fuel to travel between adjacent fueling stations and to, ultimately, complete the journey. For a project, the fuel is money. Management of fuel availability and consumption is as essential for project success as it is for operating a car. A project manager must plan a project so that enough cash is available to complete it (managing the total budget) while, at each segment of the road, enough fuel is available to arrive at the next fueling station (cash flow management).

Project activities are performed by resources that require funding. It is customary to use the term direct cost to describe the cost of resources performing project activities. Direct costs are either one-time costs, such as purchasing a piece of equipment for the project, or time dependent, such as paying a monthly salary to project team members. In addition to the direct costs of resources, other indirect costs such as overhead costs are frequently encountered. When resources are assigned to project activities, it is possible to estimate the direct cost of the project activities by multiplying the quantity of each resource required to perform the activity by the rate (cost per unit) of that resource. For example, if the daily rate of an engineer is $500 and one engineer performs an activity in two days, the cost of the engineer for that activity is $1,000. The cost of other resources, such as material, can similarly be estimated.

Indirect costs are also classified as one-time costs or time-dependent costs. For example, if a coffee machine is purchased for the project office, it is a one-time overhead cost (as the coffee machine does not perform any of the project activities). The cost of coffee capsules used with the machine is time dependent, as this cost is incurred throughout a project's duration.

In addition to direct and indirect costs, other costs may also exist. For example, if a project is financed by a loan, the cost of money (depending on the interest rate) must be considered. Since the project plan is based on estimated costs, costs associated with uncertainty must also be taken into account. For example, the cost of insurance, and, in some projects, a management reserve is added to a project budget and used to buffer the project against cost increases due to uncertainty.

6.2. Managing the Project Budget and the Project Cash Flow

Adequate financial resources must be secured for a project in order to meet its deliverables in a timely fashion and according to the scope agreed upon in the project plan. In some cases, a project is allocated all of its financial resources at the outset of the project, and the project manager does not have to advocate for funding at intermediate project checkpoints. In other cases, a project must achieve certain milestone events in order to generate income. In such cases, cash flow management is important, and the project manager, in addition to securing the financial resources for the whole project, must ensure that sufficient cash will be available in each period to cover that period's costs.

Budget management begins during a project's initiation phase. It continues throughout project execution, as a project's financial situation must be monitored and controlled continuously. In this section, we discuss financial planning, and in Chapter 8 we discuss project control.

The budgeting process is complex and requires both technical and organizational acumen on the part of the project manager. On one hand, the project management team must estimate the resources and associated costs required for each work package (WP) of the work breakdown structure (WBS). On the other hand, if a project is not budgeted correctly at the outset, then the project manager will be forced to request additional funding later on. The funding organization may not be prepared for additional funding requests, thereby potentially jeopardizing the deliverables of the project. A project manager must also be organizationally savvy and cultivate internal, influential project champions. A project manager can lean on such champions should a budget shortfall ensue and additional funding be required.

In general, the budgeting process is a hybrid of top-down and bottom-up approaches. A top-down process is one in which senior management of the organization allocates funding across various projects and functional areas, say, for the upcoming fiscal year. In practice, an organization develops multi-year budget plans. However, the current fiscal year's budget is probably most important to a project manager since this is the budget that will actually be executed by the organization. A bottom-up process is one in which the project team estimates funding required based on the WPs of the WBS, including required resources, such as subcontractors and equipment. In many organizations, the top-down and bottom-up budgets need to be reconciled through internal negotiations. Ideally, a project manager is represented in these negotiations, advocating for the project's requested funding level. In a typical organization, the reconciliation process is highly competitive, as various project managers and functional managers vie for limited and scarce resources. A project manager must prioritize the budgeting process, for, without sufficient funding, a project will fall short on either the quality or the timing of its deliverables.

Financial planning, along with scheduling, resource management, and risk management, is part of project planning. The decision of how to perform each activity (mode selection) and when to do it impact the cost of the project, its duration, resources requirements, and the value generated by the project. It is important to understand the tradeoff between the cost, schedule, performance, and risk in order to develop an optimal and balanced project plan.

In the preceding chapters, we focused on project management problems that involved optimizing the completion time of the project. In practice, a project manager must trade off scheduling and cost considerations. For example, in certain situations, it is preferable to delay a project and avoid certain costs. Consider a project that requires a certain resource that has a peak and non-peak period rate to use the resource. The project may benefit from deploying the resource in a non-peak period, although this may delay the project's completion time. In general, a project may seek to schedule revenue-generating activities as early as possible and cost-generating activities as late as possible. A project manager must recognize the time value of money. A dollar today has a higher value than a dollar tomorrow. The net present value (NPV) measurement quantifies this principle. The formula for NPV is given by:

$$NPV = \sum_{t=0}^{T} \frac{F_t}{(1+r)^t},$$

where r is the discount rate and F_t is the net cash flow associated with the project in period t. Intuitively, the NPV formula captures some of the risk associated with a project. For example, a new technology may incur significant research and development costs at the outset and promise significant revenues and profits much later in the new technology's life cycle. Since the revenues are scheduled further downstream, they are more heavily discounted than the costs which are incurred in the initial periods.

The following example illustrates a project in which a schedule delay is optimal from an NPV perspective. Consider the project network in Fig. 6.1.

For this project, let us assume that a cash payment of $5,000 must be made before activity D starts, and a cash payment of $10,000 is received when the overall project finishes (the End node is reached). The durations of the activities are given in Table 6.1. Assume a discount rate of 3% per period.

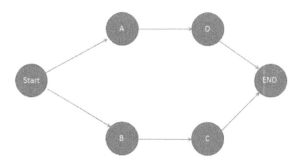

Fig. 6.1. Example to illustrate NPV of a project

Table 6.1. Duration times of activities in the example project network

Activity	Duration	Start Time	NPV
A	3	0	
B	6	0	
C	5	6	
D	7	3	$(4.58)
End	0	11	$5.06
Overall NPV			$0.48

The critical path in the network is Start–B–C–End, and the project completion time is 11. The NPV of the project is positive — $0.48 and provides value to the organization.

Now, let us consider delaying the payment that must be made before activity D starts. If activity D is pushed back to start in time period 5, then the overall project will not be completed until time period 12. The revised critical path is Start–A–D–End. The NPV, however, increased to $0.60, as shown in Table 6.2.

In practice, a project manager must be sensitive to the relative importance of cost and time. In certain projects, for example, the opening of a Broadway show, a delay in project completion is unacceptable, regardless of the additional costs that may be incurred. However, in certain projects, the stakeholders may be more indifferent as to when the project is actually completed and are more sensitive to cost, for example, the construction of a private home.

Project stakeholders are often interested in compressing the duration of a project. For example, an organization's ability to rapidly introduce a new product in the market can significantly increase the new product's profitability. A desire to decrease overall project duration time must be balanced by the costs required to achieve schedule compression. As discussed above, a project's total cost includes direct costs, overhead and indirect costs. Typically, there is an inverse relationship between an activity's direct costs and the estimated time duration of the activity. For example, a more experienced software developer can complete an activity at a faster rate than a more junior developer — but at a higher cost.

Table 6.2. NPV Increases by delaying activity D and the overall project

Activity	Duration	Start Time	NPV
A	3	0	
B	6	0	
C	5	6	
D	7	5	$(4.31)
End	0	12	$4.91
Overall NPV			$0.60

Likewise, in some instances, a project manager can reduce the duration of an activity by assigning more resources to that activity, for example, workers involved in a pick/pack/ship process in a large-scale distribution facility. A project's overhead and indirect costs are often assumed to be linearly proportional to the duration time of the overall project. For example, in a construction project, the cost of a security guard at the construction site is proportional to the length (in time) of the project. In general, as the overall duration of a project increases, the direct costs associated with the project decrease, and the indirect costs increase. This relationship is illustrated in Fig. 6.2.

We illustrate the trade-off between a project's overall duration time and its direct cost using the project network depicted in Fig. 6.3.

For each activity in Fig. 6.3, Table 6.3 provides the duration time and the marginal cost required to compress the activity by one time period. We assume that activities A and F cannot be compressed, and activities B, C, D, and E can be compressed by up to two time periods.

In order to illustrate project compression (sometimes referred to as crashing an activity), we first calculate the critical path using the "standard" ("normal") duration times in Table 6.3. The path A–C–D–F represents the critical path in this network with a project duration of 25. A "greedy" heuristic procedure is deployed to minimize the increase in total cost while reducing project duration by one time period at each iteration of the algorithm. Although activity E has the minimum marginal cost of all of the project's activities, it is not on the critical path. Therefore, reducing the time required to carry out activity E will not result in decreasing the project's duration.

Cost

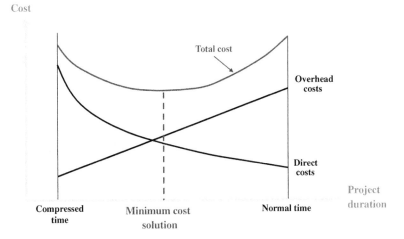

Fig. 6.2. Inverse relationship between direct and indirect costs associated with a project

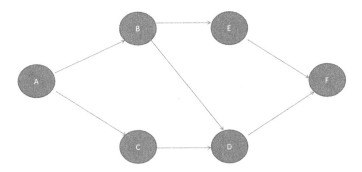

Fig. 6.3. Example project network to illustrate time/direct cost trade-off

Table 6.3. Duration times and marginal compression costs for each activity in the example network

Activity	Duration Time	Marginal Compression Cost
A	3	—
B	4	8
C	5	5
D	13	10
E	8	4
F	4	—

In practice, a project manager should focus on the critical activities in considering which activities to crash in order to reduce a project's overall completion time. As we saw from our discussion in Chapter 3 concerning uncertainty associated with project duration times in practice, a project manager is justified in crashing a non-critical activity, in practice, if that non-critical activity has a reasonable likelihood of becoming a critical activity due to uncertainty associated with activity durations.

In order to reduce the project duration from 25 to 24 in our example, the greedy heuristic would select to crash activity C. This activity is critical and has the smallest marginal cost of all the activities that lie on the critical path. By crashing the duration time of activity C from 5 to 4, total project cost increases by five units. By reducing the project duration to 24, two critical paths are now created — the incumbent A–C–D–F and the path A–B–D–F that also has a length of 24. Now, let us consider reducing the project duration from 24 to 23. If we choose to crash C since it has the minimum marginal cost, we will only reduce the length of the path A–C–D–F. The project duration would remain at 24 since the duration of the path A–B–D–F is not changed. In order to decrease the project duration from 24 to 23, we could either reduce the duration times of activities B and C (the respective activities with the smallest marginal costs on each of the two critical paths) or reduce activity D that is common to both critical paths. In the former case, total project cost increases by 8 + 5 or 13, while, in the latter case, total project cost increases by 10. Clearly, then, the heuristic selects to crash the duration time of activity D from 13 to 12, reducing the project duration from 24 to 23 in the process.

The heuristic continues by crashing the duration time of activity D from 12 to 11. Project duration decreases from 23 to 22. At this point, activity D cannot be further compressed, since each activity in the network had a technical constraint that does not allow a project manager to crash any particular activity by more than two time periods (activities A and F cannot be compressed at all). Once the heuristic exhausts its ability to compress the duration of activity D, it can choose to crash the duration times of both activities B and C and decrease project duration to 21. At this point, activity C cannot be further compressed, and the algorithm terminates. Overall, project duration, in this example, was reduced from 25 to 21 at a cost of 5 + 10 + 10 +13 = 38. Activity E was never compressed since it never appeared on any critical path.

In general, the problem of compressing a project's completion time while minimizing total cost can be formulated as a mathematical (or linear) program. However, we are not aware of any project management software that embeds a linear programming solver to optimally trade off time and cost. The greedy heuristic, described in this section, can be more easily implemented by a project manager, in practice.

We also present a variant of the time/cost trade-off problem, encountered by project managers. In certain situations, an activity may only be performed by one of several, alternative, discrete modes. Each mode represents a specific resource and includes an estimate of the duration time needed to complete each activity to which it is assigned. For example, experienced trainers can train a new sales team in a shorter duration of time than a more junior set of trainers — however, it will incur a higher cost. The time/cost trade-off with discrete mode choice is modeled by the Project Team Builder (PTB) software, as described below. Using the software, a project manager can experiment with several scenarios that deploy various combinations of the different, available modes. An optimal solution to the discrete mode choice project compression problem can be obtained by formulating and solving an integer, linear program. In practice, project managers experiment with various scenarios, rather than seeking an optimal solution via a mathematical programming approach.

6.3. Budgeting in the PTB

Financial information is presented at the scenario, activity, and resource levels and is summarized in the detailed budget of the project.

6.3.1. Pre-planning information

The following information is available as soon as the student version of PTB is loaded:

6.3.1.1 Scenario information

Clicking on the Scenario Info button under the "General Information" menu group, in the "Plan Execute Control" menu tab, opens the Scenario

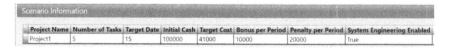

Fig. 6.4.   Scenario information

Information screen which includes the following budgeting information for each project (see Fig. 6.4):

- **Initial Cash** — The amount of cash at the beginning of the project.
- **Bonus/Period** — The bonus per period in case of early completion of the project. The bonus is awarded for each period the project is completed before the Target Date.
- **Penalty/Period** — The penalty per period in case of late completion of the project. The penalty is assessed for each period in which the project is still not completed after the Target Date.

6.3.1.2. *Task information*

A double-click on a task node in the network or on the task bar in the Gantt chart opens the task planning window (see Fig. 6.5).

Budgeting information at the task level includes:

- **Income** — The amount of cash generated at the end of the task.
- **Cost of Split** — The cost of each split (break) in the task execution (if splitting is enabled).
- **Fixed Cost** — The one-time cost necessary to perform the task in the selected mode. This cost does not depend on the task duration and the resources used to perform the task.

6.3.1.3. *Resource information*

Cost information for resources is presented in the lower part of the screen by pressing the Resource Information button under the Resource Information menu group in the "Plan Execute Control" menu tab (see Fig. 6.6).

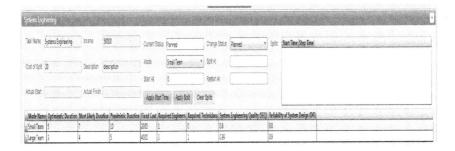

Fig. 6.5.   Task planning view

Fig. 6.6.   Resource information

The information, summarized in a table, includes the following data:

- **Cost per Period** — Per-period cost of the resource while performing a task.
- **Idle Cost per Period** — Per-period cost of the resource while not performing a task.
- **Releasing Cost** — The cost of reducing a resource's availability by one unit.
- **Assigning Cost** — The cost of increasing a resource's availability by one unit.

Some resource information and financial information is available only after the project tasks are planned, i.e., a mode is selected for each task, and a starting time is assigned.

6.3.2. *Post-planning information*

When the project tasks are planned, further information is then available. This information includes a cumulative cash flow, a periodical cash flow graph, information on actual cost and income, and a detailed budget.

6.3.2.1. *Cumulative cash flow*

By pressing the Cumulative button under the Financial Information menu group in the "Plan Execute Control" menu tab, it is possible to see the cumulative cash flow over the project duration — see Fig. 6.7.

In the cumulative cash flow chart, each bar represents the cash position at the end of the relevant period. When the cash position is positive, the bar for that period is green, and the user can continue to run the simulation from that period. When the cash position is negative, the bar for that period is red, and the simulation run will stop at that period due to bankruptcy. Additionally, the current time period is depicted by a vertical line. All information to the left of the line shows what actually happened in the project. Information to the right of the line shows what is expected to happen.

6.3.2.2. *Periodical cash flow*

By pressing the Periodical button under the Financial Information menu group in the "Plan Execute Control" menu tab, it is possible to see the per-period cash flow view — see Fig. 6.8.

In this view, for each period, a user can see the expected cash flow. Green colored bars depict periods with a positive cash flow, while red ones depict a negative cash flow. A project manager gains insight as to which periods in a project's time horizon are potentially problematic due to a net

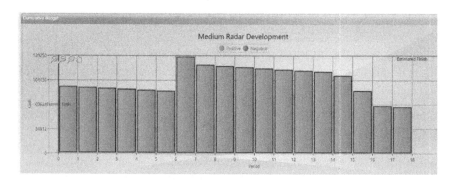

Fig. 6.7. Cumulative cash flow

outflow of cash in that period. Likewise, a project manager can discover those periods where a project is expected to bring revenue into the organization. These insights assist a project manager in internal communications and managing stakeholders' expectations.

Additionally, the current time period is depicted by a vertical line. All information to the left of the line shows what actually happened in the project. Information to the right of the line shows what is expected to happen.

6.3.2.3. *Detailed budget*

By pressing the "Detailed" button under the Financial Information menu group in the "Plan Execute Control" menu tab, a user may inspect the detailed budget information — see Fig. 6.9. The detailed budget table lists costs and income for each period of the project. Entries in the table are actual costs and income up to the current simulation period (highlighted in light blue) and planned (or forecasted) costs and income from the current period to the planned simulation end period. At the end of the simulation

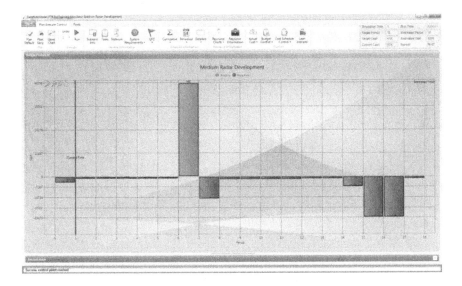

Fig. 6.8. Per-period cash flow

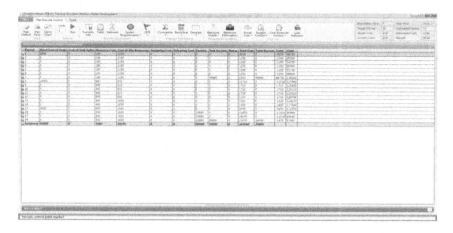

Fig. 6.9. Detailed budget view

Actual Cost and Income Medium Radar Development	
Fixed Cost of Tasks	12000
Resources Cost	3400
Idle Cost of Resources	10480
Penalty	0
Total Cost	25880
Tasks Income	50000
Bonus	0
Total Income	50000

Fig. 6.10. Actual cost/income report

run, the detailed budget table lists the actual periodic costs and income for each period of the project. Additionally, the last line in the chart displays a summary.

6.3.2.4. *Actual cost/income report*

The Actual Cost/Income report contains actual income and costs for any given point in the simulation (see Fig. 6.10).

6.4. Summary

A project budget communicates to project team members and stakeholders the funding allocation plan for the project. A good budget should be well integrated with the schedule and resource management. A project manager must be organizationally savvy to procure sufficient funding in order to deliver project milestones on time and according to the features and scope that were described in the project proposal.

Chapter 7

Risk Management

7.1. The Sources and Nature of Uncertainty and Risk

The non-repetitive nature of projects complicates the process of forecasting information needed for project planning, such as activity duration, resource needs/availability, and costs. Inaccuracy of estimates is one of the leading causes of project failures. It is also difficult to predict events that might take place during a project's life cycle and how these events may affect project success in satisfying stakeholders' needs and expectations or a project team's ability to satisfy time, cost, and requirement constraints. For example, most economists failed to predict the banking crisis in the US in 2007–2008 that precipitated a contraction of the overall economy. The presence of risk is part of the nature of projects, and the need to manage such risks has motivated development of a terminology and a methodology for risk management.

A common definition of risk, in the area of project management, is an (adverse) event that has a positive probability to occur and that has a negative impact on project success. Risk events are classified in several ways:

(1) **Internal vs. External Risks** — Internal risks are events related to the project team and to the organizations involved in the project. External risks are related to organizations not participating in the project and to the political, economic, and technological environment in which the project is performed.

(2) **Technological vs. Other Risks** — Technological risks are related to the technologies used by the project. The maturity and stability of these technologies impact the probability of success of the product and services delivered by the project. Non-technological risks are typically economic or political in nature.

(3) **Known Unknown vs. Unknown Unknown** — Known unknown are risk events that took place in the past. A project manager can estimate the probability of occurrence of such an event and its expected impact on project cost, schedule, and performance. For example, in the research and development phase of a new pharmaceutical product, it is known by scientists and product developers that the new chemical compound may fail in Phase III clinical trials when it is tested with human patients. Unknown unknown risks are risk events that did not take place in the past. These are the result of knowledge gaps of the project manager and the project management team. In the pharmaceutical example, although it is known that a new compound may fail in clinical trials, the gamut of adverse events that may occur may not be fully known (that is, a compound may fail due to an adverse condition that had not previously occurred with other similar compounds).

Risk classification is important, as each class of risk should be assigned to an "owner", that is a member of the project team who is an expert in the relevant area and can manage that risk. The risk owner is responsible and accountable for the outcome of risk management efforts in the assigned domain area.

7.2. Risk Management Methodology

To help project managers and their teams deal with uncertainty and risk, a project risk management methodology was developed. The methodology includes processes, tools, and techniques that support the identification of risks, the qualitative and quantitative analysis of risks, and the decision if, when, and what to do about risks based on the analysis. This last decision is mostly a choice between dealing with the risk event before it takes place (also known as proactive risk management or mitigation) and the alternative of waiting for the risk event to occur and only then dealing with it (also known as reactive risk management). The decision whether to mitigate a risk or not depends not only on the classification of the risk event but also on the probability of its occurrence and the impact it might have on the project. In many projects, high-risk events (high probability and high impact) are mitigated, while, for other risk events a reactive approach is selected. A complementary methodology was developed to help project managers and project teams monitor and control the risks that are not mitigated (also known as residual risks) throughout the project life cycle. Project monitoring and control methodologies, tools, and techniques are discussed in the next chapter.

Risk management starts with an effort to identify risk events that might have a negative impact on the project. A good starting point is a data base of past projects that contains details of risk events that took place in the past, their frequency of occurrence, and their impact on the project. If such a database does not exist, expert opinion based on the knowledge of experienced project managers and project team members might be used. The end result is a list of risk events that might take place in the project along with an estimate of their probability of occurrence and their expected impact on cost, schedule, and performance. In some projects, it is possible to identify symptoms associated with some risks. An experienced project manager learns to recognize certain signals that are precursors to a negative event looming on the project horizon. These signals serve as an early warning and can be used by a project manager to trigger certain contingency plans or other preemptive actions that mitigate or blunt the impact of risk events.

The risks identified are analyzed by using quantitative and qualitative tools aimed at ranking these risk events according to their probability of occurrence and their impact on the project. The analysis results in an ordered list, ranking risk events with high impact — high probability risks — at the top. The next step of the analysis focuses on the question of whether a proactive or reactive approach should be adopted for each risk event. A general rule is based on a cost/benefit analysis — comparing the cost of mitigating a specific risk event and the benefit of doing so. If both cost and benefit can be expressed in monetary terms, the comparison is relatively easy. Otherwise, the question revolves around the stakeholders' attitude toward risk, the impact of the risk event should it take place, and the possible mitigation strategies and their costs.

Risk mitigation can take many forms. An extreme approach is to avoid a risk completely by selecting another alternative that is not impacted by the risk event, for example, selecting a mature technology instead of a new technology although the new technology has potentially better performance (but higher risk). Mitigation is also possible by sharing the risk with a subcontractor, a supplier, a partner, or even with the customer. A typical example is purchasing insurance and sharing the risk with the insurance company.

For each type of risk, a proper mitigation strategy must be developed. For example, the risk involved in developing a new technological solution can be mitigated by parallel development of two competing technologies by two independent teams, assuming that the probability of failure of both teams is smaller than the probability that a single development team will fail. This risk management strategy was routinely adhered to by such technology companies as IBM, which typically launched multiple project teams in pursuit of a new, breakthrough, technology.

When a reactive approach is selected for some risk events, an effort to identify symptoms and to monitor those symptoms may be appropriate. In some cases, it is possible to prepare contingency plans so that a backup plan is automatically triggered if a certain symptom is encountered. For example, if wind gusts exceed 50 miles per hour, then backup plans to secure a construction site, due to advancing, inclement weather conditions, are automatically put into action. If symptoms are not present and mitigation is not a good option, buffers may be used to protect a project against some risk events. A time buffer is created by developing a project schedule that finishes before the project due date. If the project is late compared to the planned schedule, some spare time (buffer) is available to protect the project from missing its due date. Likewise, a buffer can be added to the budget (also known as Management Reserve) to cover the costs of risk events that might take place. Other types of buffers are used as well, for example, a resource buffer is used when a resource has a significant probability of not being available when needed (e.g., a machine that suffers from frequent breakdowns — in this case, an extra machine of the same type may be rented in critical times to protect the overall project's schedule from a machine breakdown).

Inevitably, despite a project management team's planning and preparing for risks, changes to a project plan arise in practice. Changes to a project plan are almost a given due to the large number of internal and external factors that touch a project. Change management can, therefore, be viewed as a complementary activity to risk management. A change management process should be developed, documented, and communicated to a project team and its stakeholders. It is critical for a formal process to be in place to handle changes to a project plan. Otherwise, on-the-fly and ad hoc decision making could result in even further setbacks to a project delivery schedule, in addition to increasing the likelihood of tensions arising within a project team or among a project's stakeholders. In a change management process, a project team decides on a process for evaluating proposed changes to a project. Typically, changes should be submitted in writing and include an assessment of the costs and benefits of the proposed change. A change request should also include an assessment of the proposed change on resources and the project's delivery schedule.

A project's organizational structure typically includes a project Change Control Board (CCB), consisting of key stakeholders such as the project manager, senior management, and a systems engineer. The CCB is ultimately responsible for deciding on whether to incorporate a proposed change request into the overall project plan. In certain cases, the magnitude of the change request, in terms of its impact on the project, may not require the attention of the full CCB. In these cases, the project management office can decide on the viability of a change request. If a change request is approved, the work packages that are affected by the change must be updated in the overall project plan. This step involves updating the cost, timing, and resources associated with one or more project activities. In practice, documentation of all change requests is a best practice. A project team, upon termination of a project, will want to understand and explain deviations in cost, schedule, and scope in the delivered project vs. the originally approved project plan. If changes are properly documented, then conducting a project "postmortem" is facilitated.

There are two quantitative tools that may be helpful to a project manager in assessing risk. A *tornado diagram* depicts a sensitivity analysis of underlying input variables that are tied to project costs. Each input variable, such as the direct cost of each resource type, is varied — one-by-one — and its impact on overall project cost is estimated. In constructing a tornado diagram, a project manager must consider a wide range of scenarios to include low-end and high-end estimates of input variable costs. For example, in the sales force expansion example discussed earlier, the cost of management science resources may vary significantly. If senior management rapidly approves an initial sales force structure and expansion plan, then management science costs, associated with developing the structure and sales force territory alignment, are minimal. However, if multiple scenarios need to be fleshed out, then management science costs — which are correlated with the number of sales force structure scenarios that are examined — increase. The value of a tornado diagram is that it reveals the most sensitive input parameters associated with a project. A project manager, for example, can rank resource types, using a tornado diagram, by their level of impact on overall, project costs.

An example of a tornado diagram is provided below in Fig. 7.1. In the sales force expansion project example, let us assume that the overall project is expected to cost $2MM. Several of the tasks, involving four resource types, were judged to have some level of variability associated with their duration times. In order to test the sensitivity of overall project cost to changes in the usage of certain key resources, a project manager

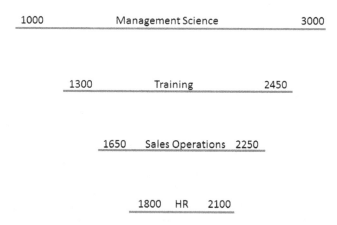

Fig. 7.1. Example of a tornado diagram

can vary each resource's usage from a low to high estimate while holding all other factors constant. For both the low and high estimates, total overall project cost is calculated, as depicted in Fig. 7.1 (change in project costs is displayed in 1,000s). In this example, management science costs may vary from $1MM to $3MM, depending on how much of this resource is actually required.

A *sensitivity chart*, unlike a tornado diagram, considers changes in all of a project's input variables simultaneously. A project manager, using, say, Monte Carlo simulation, can choose a point estimate for each input parameter over a range of possible outcomes and an assumed, underlying probability distribution. Given a particular instance of input parameter values, the simulation can provide a point estimate of the overall project cost. A simulation may be executed for several hundred (or several thousand) iterations to obtain a sensitivity chart. For each input parameter, a correlation coefficient can be calculated to determine those input parameters that have the greatest impact on the overall project cost.

An example of a sensitivity chart, based on the sales force expansion project example, is given in Fig. 7.2. The sensitivity chart depicts that overall project costs are most highly correlated with changes in management science costs. The project manager, in this case, should

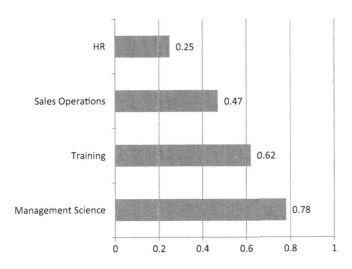

Fig. 7.2. Example of sensitivity chart

most carefully track and monitor management science resource usage (and associated costs) in order to best manage the overall project budget.

7.3. Risk Management in the PTB

There are two sources of risk in PTB scenarios:

(1) **Risk Associated with the Duration of Activities** — The duration of each activity is a function of the resources assigned to it (the mode selected). The duration of some activities can be accurately estimated, and the level of uncertainty is low enough to be ignored. In cases where the estimated duration is not sufficiently accurate, activity duration is modeled by a three-point estimate (the optimistic or shortest duration, the most likely duration, and the pessimistic or the longest duration). The actual duration is randomly generated during a simulation run from a triangle distribution with the above three parameters, see Fig. 7.3.

(2) **Risk Associated with the Availability of Resources** — This is depicted as the Show up Probability. It is 100% in situations where the risk is low enough to be ignored, or it takes a value <100% when the risk of resource no show is substantial (for example, a worker is busy on another task in a matrix organization or a machine tends to break-down). The show up probability is provided by pressing the Resource Information button under the Resource Information menu group in the "Plan Execute Control" menu tab (refer to Fig. 5.1 in Chapter 5).

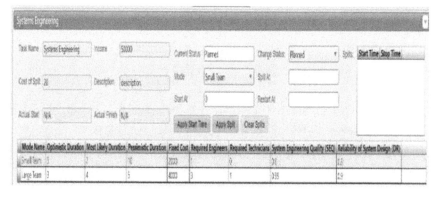

Fig. 7.3.   Three points estimate activity duration

In PTB, several types of buffers can be implicitly created by a user to manage risk:

- A time buffer is created if the project schedule is shorter than the time available from project start to its due date.
- A management reserve is created if the project planned cost is lower than the required cost.
- A resource buffer is created if the number of resource units available at any given time is greater than the number required according to the project plan.

In case of resource no show, it is possible to split an activity — to stop its execution for one or more periods and to continue execution when enough resources are available.

7.4. Summary

Projects are performed in an uncertain environment due to their non-repetitive nature and the use of cutting-edge technologies. Risk management methodologies can help a project manager and a project team identify, analyze, and manage risks by adopting a proactive, a reactive, or a mixed strategy. In the next chapter, we discuss the benefits of project monitoring and control, activities that complement risk management.

Chapter 8

Project Integration — Planning, Executing Monitoring, and Controlling the Project

8.1. What is Project Integration?

The text has so far focused on specific aspects (or building blocks) of project management. Chapters 1 and 2 presented an introduction to project management and an introduction to simulation-based training. Chapters 3–7 presented a set of tools and techniques that may be used to support a project manager and a project management team in the following areas:

Chapter 3 — Stakeholders requirements and value
Chapter 4 — Scheduling
Chapter 5 — Resource management
Chapter 6 — Budgeting
Chapter 7 — Risk management

These building blocks are dependent on each other, and trade-offs exist between them. For example, in many projects, it is possible to reduce the cost and duration by reducing project scope. Alternatively, project duration can be reduced by adding resources to some activities, thereby increasing the project's direct cost. We also described how mode selection for project activities affect simultaneously the cost, duration, risk, and benefit of a project.

A project manager must consider all aspects of a project and the inter-relationships between a project's various work streams. When we refer to project integration, we include the composite and holistic strategy that a project manager must develop in order to guide a project in its entirety. A decision with regard to, say, costs or resources that, on the surface, may only affect a particular project module at the outset of a project may have longer-term implications and consequences that could affect the project in a later time period. Integration is aimed at satisfying stakeholder needs and expectations by generating a high-value and low-waste plan and executing it successfully.

Integration begins with project initiation. A decision to start a new project must take into account the cost, duration, risk, and benefit of the project simultaneously. Integration continues during the detailed project planning phase when activity modes are selected, activities are scheduled, and resources are allocated. Integration extends to project execution when a risk event may occur and a corrective action or even replanning of a substantive project workstream is needed as part of the monitoring and control process.

When a new project is initiated, needs and expectations are translated into project goals and constraints, including the project due date (or target finish date), its target cost and budget, and key deliverables. Goals and constraints are used as a basis for the development of alternatives (remember that one alternative is always not to do the project or a "no go" decision). Alternatives may be based on redesign and modifications of existing solutions or development of new solutions from scratch. Each alternative is evaluated based on cost, duration, risk, and benefit of the associated project plan. The end result is an efficient frontier of all the alternative project plans that are not dominated by other alternatives. For the medium radar development example, there are 32 possible combinations or mode selection alternatives (5 activities with 2 possible modes for each activity — 2 to the power of 5 is 32). Of the 32 alternatives, only 12 are feasible — they do not violate any constraint, and only 2 are efficient as they dominate the other 10 alternatives. An alternative is dominated if there exists another alternative that is better in at least one performance measure and not worse in any other performance measure (in the radar example, the performance measures are range,

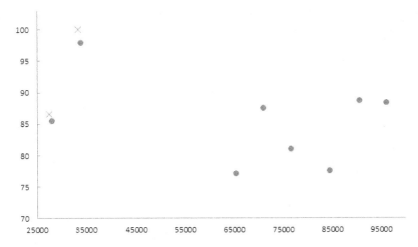

Fig. 8.1. The efficient frontier of the medium difficulty radar example

quality, reliability, cost, and duration of the project). The efficient frontier for the radar development project is illustrated in Fig. 8.1. The blue dots represent feasible solutions, while the red crosses represent the efficient solutions.

In the efficient frontier of the medium difficulty radar example, there are two efficient alternatives.

8.2. Developing an Integrated Project Plan

There are three approaches to the development of an integrated project plan:

(1) Developing a feasible plan that is good enough — also known as a heuristic planning approach.
(2) Developing a plan that is feasible and lies on the efficient frontier.
(3) Developing all feasible project plans that lie on the efficient frontier and using trade-off analysis to select the most appropriate plan.

Due to the mathematical complexity of the second and third approaches, in most projects, the first approach is used.

A simple heuristic starts with a default plan, frequently a plan based on selecting the least expensive mode for each activity and planning the project using scheduling, resource allocation, and budgeting tools that were presented in earlier chapters. The first step is to ensure that the plan is feasible — it does not violate any of the project constraints. Once a feasible plan is developed, the next step is to improve it as much as possible.

Consider, for example, the simple radar development project. The schedule resulting from the default plan is presented in Fig. 8.2.

The project duration, under the default plan, is 18 periods, while the required duration is 16 periods. The critical activities are systems engineering, antenna design, and integration and testing, as shown in Fig. 8.2. By changing the mode of systems engineering from a small team to a large team and using the early start schedule (Plan Early option in PTB), a project manager can reduce the project duration to 15 periods, as shown in Fig. 8.3.

The project duration is now feasible, and the next step is to check the product requirements. The quality requirements screen in Fig. 8.4 reveals that the reliability of the radar is 65.61, which exceeds the required score of 65. Therefore, the score for reliability is 100. The quality score is 73.74, very close to the required 75, and, therefore, there is very little room for improvement. The range, however, is only 11.07 miles, while the required range is 12 miles. The score of the range is only 53.5 out of a 100 and can be substantially improved.

In order to improve the range, a project manager can inspect the parameters used to calculate the range in the QFD matrix in Fig. 8.5.

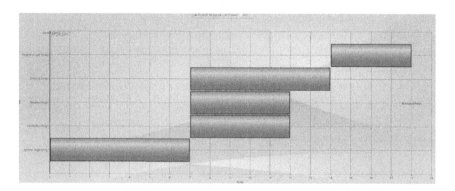

Fig. 8.2. A schedule for the default plan of the simple radar development project

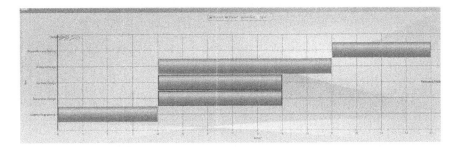

Fig. 8.3. A 15-period schedule for the radar development project

Name	Formula	Importance	Minimum Value	Desired Value	Maximum Value	Best Mode	Evaluation	Project	Score
Quality Requirements									
⊙ Project1									
Range	Pow([TP]*[RS]*[AG],0.25)	7	10	12	NA	Maximum	11.07	Project1	53.5
Quality	[SEQ]*[QT]*[QR]*[QA]*[QI]*100	8	0	75	NA	Maximum	73.74	Project1	98.32
Reliability	[AR]*[IR]*[TR]*[RR]*100	6	0	65	NA	Maximum	65.61	Project1	(x)

Fig. 8.4. Quality requirements for the radar development project

What	Range	Quality	Reliability
QFD			
⊙ Project1			
Formula	Pow([TP]*[RS]*[AG],0.25)	[SEQ]*[QT]*[QR]*[QA]*[QI]*100	[AR]*[IR]*[TR]*[RR]*100
Systems Engineering		SEQ	
Transmitter Design	TP	QT	TR
Receiver Design	RS	QR	RR
Antenna Design	AG	QA	AR
Integration and Testing		QI	IR

Fig. 8.5. QFD matrix for the radar development project

From the QFD matrix, it is clear that the modes selected for three activities impact the range:

- Transmitter design impacts the transmitter power TP,
- Receiver design impacts the receiver sensitivity RS,
- Antenna design impacts the antenna gain AG.

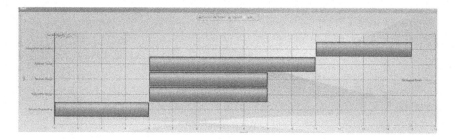

Fig. 8.6. The schedule after changing the mode of antenna design

Using PTB, a project manager can easily evaluate the impact of changing the mode of each of these activities by switching the modes of the transmitter design, the receiver design, and the antenna design, one at a time, and evaluating the resulting cost, duration, and benefit. By changing the mode for antenna design, a project manager can improve the range while completing the project on time at a relatively low incremental cost, as shown in Fig. 8.6.

A project manager can readily implement this trial-and-error heuristic with the PTB, as the impact of changing activity modes is easily evaluated.

8.3. Project Monitoring and Control — The Impact of Uncertainty of Project Integration

When the level of uncertainty, for example, in an activity's expected duration time or in a machine's probability of avoiding a breakdown, is too high to be ignored, development of a good, initial plan is only a first step in management of a project. The associated project plan needs to consider risk, and the project must be monitored and controlled throughout its execution to identify deviations from plan and to take corrective actions when needed.

Project monitoring and control is based on a comparison between a project plan and the actual progress of the associated project during its execution. Any deviation between plan and actual progress should be analyzed to find the cause of the deviation and its impact. Based on an analysis of deviations from plan, decisions are made regarding the need to take corrective action to bring the project back on track. There is a wide spectrum of possible decisions. At one extreme, the deviation might be too small to justify a corrective action, and the project manager may decide to take no corrective action. At the other extreme, the deviation may be so significant, requiring that the project be terminated. In between the two extremes, there are many possible decisions available to a project manager, such as modifying project scope, changing the schedule or the budget, altering the resource mix, or the mode, of some activities, or making changes in personnel.

To assist the project management team during the execution phase, a comparison between planned and actual performance is performed. This comparison, which is supported by the PTB software, is done each period for each activity, and a variety of performance metrics are reviewed. A typical performance measure is the duration of activities — a comparison between the planned duration and the actual duration. Related performance measures are the start time and finish time of project activities. Cost is also frequently used as a performance measure. A comparison between the planned cost of an activity and the actual cost, on either a per-period or cumulative basis, may help a project manager identify deviations in cost and trigger root cause analysis and, sometimes, even corrective actions.

8.4. Project Integration in the PTB

8.4.1. *Project planning*

Once a scenario is opened, a user can begin to plan the project, as described in Chapter 4. A default project plan can be constructed by setting all tasks to start at their earliest possible start time. Tools for task planning were described in Chapter 4, including mode selection and splitting of tasks.

Tools for resource management were described in Chapter 5. A project manager can assign resources to a project for its entirety or for a particular window of time. The PTB software enables a project manager to experiment with different resource scenarios, for example, adding more resources or changing the start times of tasks that require certain scarce resources.

8.4.2. Running the simulation

8.4.2.1. The run command

After planning all tasks, it is possible to run the simulation by clicking on the "**Run**" button. This advances the simulation time by the number of periods specified in the Units field. By default, this is one time period (see Fig. 8.7).

The simulation continues to advance until project termination is achieved (that is, all tasks are completed), unless an infeasibility condition is encountered. As the time counter in the simulation advances, the cash position changes, and tasks are performed according to the schedule.

The simulation run would be interrupted in the following cases:

1. **Undefined Task** — When a task that can start (i.e., it has no predecessors or all its predecessors are completed) is not planned. A user must select a mode for each task or may select Plan Default, prior to simulating the task (see Section 4.2 for a discussion on planning a task).
2. **Resource Violation** — Resource requirements for the run period are greater than the availability of that resource.
3. **Budget Violation** — Cash requirements for the run period are greater than the availability of cash.

PTB displays a message in each of the above cases (see Fig. 8.8).

Fig. 8.7.   Run and Units buttons

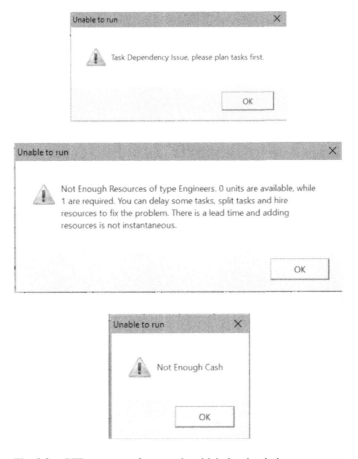

Fig. 8.8. PTB messages for cases in which the simulation cannot run

Upon completion of the project, all tasks in the network view change color to depict completion. A summary of the session is presented (Fig. 8.9).

- While running the simulation, actual task durations are generated, and the planned task time is changed to the actual task time. In stochastic scenarios, actual values are generated randomly and may differ from planned values.
- A user might change the task start time for tasks that did not start yet in order to satisfy resource or cash limitations. Changes are performed by updating **Start At** in the task planning window, described in Chapter 4.

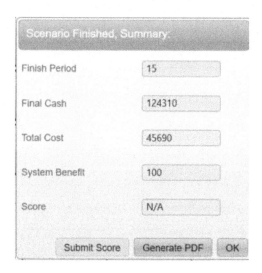

Fig. 8.9. Project completion summary view

- While running the simulation, in some scenarios, the actual availability of resources is randomly generated. In scenarios in which a resource's availability shows a probability of less than 100%, it might be necessary to stop the execution of the task until enough units of the resource are available (to split the task). A project manager, in real-world applications, must split a task if it is in process (already started but not finished), and the number of resource units available is less than the number of resource units required to perform the task. This is done by the Split function in the task planning window, described in Chapter 4.
- In some scenarios, a user might change the level of resources available by using the **Assign/Release** commands as explained below.

8.5. Assigning and Releasing Resources

A project manager may change the level of certain resources within preset minimum and maximum levels in order to reach optimal performance. A lead time (greater than 0) is associated with adding and dropping resources. The lead time models real-world conditions in which resources

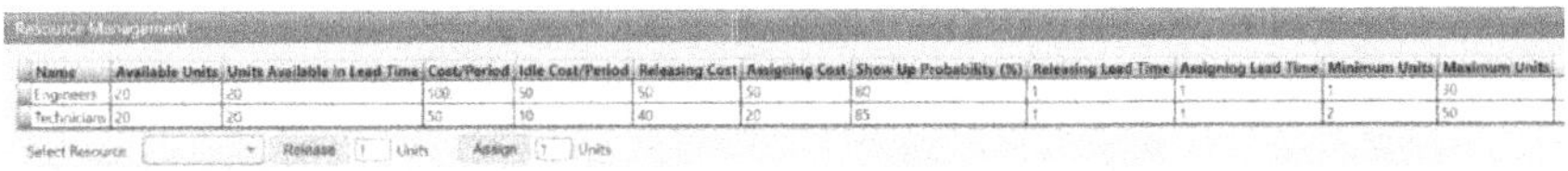

Fig. 8.10. Assign/release resources

cannot be instantaneously added or removed from a project. Lead times are provided by using the manage resource screen (see Fig. 8.10).

To assign or release units of a resource, a user selects the desired resource type by clicking on the "Select Resource" button in the resource management screen. The cost of assigning or releasing a resource is found in the manage resources screen. Although a cost is typically incurred if the level of a resource is changed, it might be advantageous in order to complete a project in a more timely fashion (adding resources) or to minimize overall cost (although releasing resources incurs a cost, a project avoids costs associated with having to pay idle resources).

8.6. Project Control

Project performance, including the financial situation, should be monitored and controlled. PTB supports project control using three control reports: Actual Cost, Budget Control, and Cost Schedule Control (see Fig. 8.11).

The control reports are accessible through the **Plan Execute Control menu,** under the "Control" menu group (see Fig. 8.11). The control display includes two levels: the scenario level and the project level. In case there is only one project in a scenario, only one level is displayed. In the Cost Schedule control, the scenario-level reports take into account all costs and income (for example, the cost of idle resources). The project-level reports take into account only costs and income that are related directly to the specific project.

8.7. Actual Cost/Income Report

The Actual Cost/Income report contains the actual income and costs associated with the last project time period that was simulated by

Fig. 8.11.   Control menu group

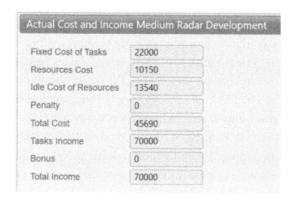

Fig. 8.12.   Actual Cost/Income report

the PTB. The report can be viewed at any time during project execution (see Fig. 8.12) by clicking on Actual Cost.

8.8. Budget Control Table

The Budget Control table presents planned vs. actual monetary performance, by time period and cumulative over a project's life cycle (see Fig. 8.13).

8.9. Cost Schedule Control

The Cost Schedule Control table presents a summary of the planned and actual duration and cost of the tasks (see Fig. 8.14).

8.10. Summary

Project integration involves linking all of the various, seemingly disparate, modules and workstreams of a project. A project manager and the project

Budget Control Medium Radar Development

Period	Planned Cost	Actual Cost	Planned Income	Actual Income	Planned Total	Actual Total
1	5390	5390	0	0	-5390	-5390
2	1390	1390	0	0	-1390	-1390
3	1390	1390	0	0	-1390	-1390
4	1390	1390	50000	50000	48610	48610
5	15810	15810	0	0	-15810	-15810
6	1810	1810	0	0	-1810	-1810
7	1810	1810	0	0	-1810	-1810
8	1810	1810	0	0	-1810	-1810
9	1810	1810	0	0	-1810	-1810
10	1530	1670	0	0	-1530	-1670
11	1530	1530	0	0	-1530	-1530
12	5470	5470	0	0	-5470	-5470
13	1470	1470	0	0	-1470	-1470
14	1470	1470	0	0	-1470	-1470
15	1470	1470	20000	20000	18530	18530

Fig. 8.13. Budget control table

Cost Schedule Control Medium Radar Development

Task Name	Task Status	Selected Mode	Planned Duration	Actual Duration	Planned Cost	Actual Cost
Systems Engineering	Finished	Large Team	4	4	5400	5400
Transmitter Design	Finished	Reengineer	5	5	6250	6250
Receiver Design	Finished	Reengineer	5	6	3250	3500
Antenna Design	Finished	New Design	7	7	11200	11200
Integration and Testing	Finished	In-House	4	4	5800	5800

Fig. 8.14. Cost schedule control table

management team are essential in this task, as they are uniquely positioned to monitor the various work packages of a project. Furthermore, they are uniquely qualified to understand the importance and priority of each project's work package and the interrelationship of work packages. This knowledge provides the project management team with a unique ability to evaluate trade-offs between schedule, cost, project scope, and risks. The PTB software supports a project management team in its integration effort, as it enables project managers to efficiently quantify and measure performance trade-offs under various assumptions and scenarios.

Chapter 9

Integration of Simulation-Based Training in Project Management Courses

9.1. Introduction

Simulation-based training, using Project Team Builder (PTB) software, has been extensively used in project management courses around the world. This chapter surveys six examples of how the PTB tool has been used to teach project management in different countries and continents.

9.2. NORTH AMERICA: Columbia University

Moshe Rosenwein, Columbia University, New York, USA
Project management has been taught at the School of Engineering, Columbia University in New York City, for almost 10 years. The course typically attracts close to 100 students who are divided roughly 50/50 between upper-class undergraduates and graduate students. The course is offered by the Department of Industrial Engineering and Operations Research (IE/OR), although students majoring in other disciplines also enroll. In general, most of the students have limited work experience and little exposure to project management. Typically, approximately 10 students participate in the course via online learning. These students tend to have richer work experience, and some are familiar with the complexities of project management.

Since the course is offered by the School of Engineering, the syllabus emphasizes quantitative methods and models that are used to support Project Management, such as Critical Path Method (CPM) and Program Evaluation and Review Technique (PERT). The course applies advanced operations research techniques, such as mathematical programming and simulation to project management.

Simulation-based training was introduced over time into the Columbia course. Specifically, the instructor and the students were given access to the Project Team Builder (PTB) software. For the instructor, the PTB software represented an opportunity to demonstrate the theoretical and conceptual aspects of the course material. For example, the sales force expansion project, which was described in Chapter 2, was presented to the class. The instructor demonstrated that using one mode of management science resources, versus an alternative mode, resulted in early project completion — but at a higher cost.

The PTB software enabled the students to create a project of their own, rather than only working on projects that were assigned as homework problems or business cases. Given the varied backgrounds of the students, the range of project applications was quite impressive. Some examples included:

- Manufacturing of consumer electronics to be used in an urban transportation system.
- Event planning, such as hosting a charity auction or an intramural soccer tournament.
- Building construction and renovation.
- Software development.
- New product introduction such as producing beer using new brewing formulas.

One student remarked that "It was a unique experience to be in a role which allowed us to demonstrate a holistic understanding of the material. We got to pick our team, design a project, and figure out how to optimize its execution."

The students, working in small teams of 2–3 students, used the PTB software to model and simulate their project. They were able to evaluate different scenarios involving trade-offs of cost, schedule and resource usage. Students presented their projects, using Microsoft PowerPoint, to the class. Student feedback was positive. For example, "the software allowed the material of the course to come to life. It was very stimulating to see how all the teams approached their projects. It allowed us to see different applications in the course material and understand its versatility."

In addition to gaining some experience with a project of their own (as opposed to working on projects that were developed by either the instructor or external business cases), students gained insight into the practice and art of project management. Students appreciated the empirical nature of the discipline and began to develop a deeper understanding of the complexities involved in a project manager's decision process.

9.3. SOUTH AMERICA: Post-Graduate School at Universidad San Ignacio de Loyola (EPG USIL)

Luis A. Chepote, Universidad San Ignacio de Loyola, Lima, Peru
For the past six years, the EPG USIL — The Post Graduate School at Universidad San Ignacio de Loyola — has been offering a Master's Program in Entrepreneurial Sciences with a major in project management. Located in Lima, Peru and with branches in Arequipa and Cusco, the EPG USIL project management major attracts participants from an array of industry sectors and professional backgrounds, such as business administration, computer science, engineering, law and the military. It is not unusual to have a class project team that consists of a lawyer working for a construction company, a submarine Navy officer, and a software development leader.

The project management major focuses on developing the knowledge and skills required to manage one or various initiatives, using a selected bibliography, case studies, and workshops. All participants are professionals with more than two years of work experience. Several participants have project management experience and seek PMP Certification while others are interested in acquiring a body of knowledge useful for their professional development.

A simulation-based teaching (SBT) approach was initially introduced into the project management curriculum as a pilot. From the pilot experience, the instructors learned that students could be "up and running" with real-world project scenarios after only one class session. The PTB simulation tool was the software selected, and a Spanish version of the tool's screens, reports and online help documentation was created.

Several project management courses make use of the PTB Simulator to address particular concepts, tools or techniques and to develop hands-on training while planning and executing a project. The use of the simulator complements lecture material that emphasizes concepts and process descriptions. In the simulator, variables such as scope, time, costs, resources, risks or cash flow are not static nor are they independent of each other. They all have values that can be estimated, planned, and controlled, as the project advances and decisions are made. Concepts like "listen to the customer" can be implemented using the Quality Function Deployment feature in the PTB. Students can propose alternative project plans or solutions to business and engineering problems using PTB features, such as stochastic durations, fixed and variable costs and resource availability and constraints. Variability, such as stochastic duration times of tasks, and constraints, such as cash flow limits, are aspects of a project that are inherently challenging for project managers in the real-world during the execution of a project. Students gain experience in real-world decision making by using the PTB.

In advanced project management courses, some of the PTB scenarios that have been constructed include design and construction of a synthetic soccer field, development of software for fishing fleet management, and remodeling the duty-free area in Peru's international airport.

The PTB software is used in a number of courses in the project management major track. In the introductory project management courses, many of the scenarios that accompany the software are assigned as exercises to students to test their ability to apply project management concepts. In the more advanced courses, the more scientifically-oriented students can apply Monte Carlo simulation for project risk analysis or determining the probability of a particular task becoming critical.

Student surveys reflect a high level of student engagement and interest. In some of the advanced project management classes, teams of students compete to have the most successful project. This healthy competition is stimulating and leads to an enhanced learning experience. Students gain deeper insights into project management fundamentals through the competitive team exercises. In general, an SBT tool provides instantaneous feedback to students concerning the impact of their decisions.

Use of SBT is expanding at EPG USIL and has been introduced in two undergraduate project management courses. Although these students do not have prior business or engineering experience, the use of an interactive software tool has proven to attract their attention and generate interest in the subject matter.

9.4. EUROPE: University of Nicosia

Angelika Kokkinaki, University of Nicosia, Nicosia, Cyprus

The home campus of the University of Nicosia (UNic) is in Nicosia, the capital city of the Republic of Cyprus, a Mediterranean island state. The University of Nicosia is the largest research university in Cyprus in terms of the number of students. In alignment with UNic's strategic orientation, student-centered methodologies are regularly employed. Simulation-based Learning is extensively used in postgraduate level courses. It is often found in the MBA curricula, including project management courses.

Within this context, students who interact with a simulation environment have access to an abstraction of a real-life situation in which operations can be carried out and their effects represented in the resulting simulation setting. It was observed that using simulation software as a training tool has several positive aspects. One of them is related to the realistic and dynamic situation with which students interact, and this contributes to a higher degree of engagement with the course content than that achieved through traditional lecturer-centered education. It is also interesting and inspiring for students to see the consequences of their decisions directly. The real-time feedback reinforces the students' experiential learning attitudes. When simulation cases are assigned as a team project, they may be used to improve teamwork and collaborative decision making. Finally, Simulation-based Learning can be incorporated in conventional face-to-face educational settings, as well as in online courses.

The University of Nicosia started using the PTB Training Simulation software in project management courses in 2014. The lead lecturer had sought a project management simulation tool as she expected that its use would improve learning of project management concepts and methods. It was also expected to contribute to advancing students' analytical and problem-solving skills in the context of project management. A main consideration for the selection of this particular product was its flexibility regarding student learning outcomes. Due to the fact that PTB is a scenario-based simulation and the scenarios provided with the software are developed to represent project management problems with various levels of difficulty, it is possible to customize its use for different target audiences. Scenarios of varying difficulty (low, medium, high) are selected for different cohorts of students. This flexibility has enabled instructors to use the same simulation software for undergraduate students (who only have an introductory project management course in their program) and for postgraduate students who take an advanced project management course as an elective in their specialization. PTB Training Simulation has also been employed by students who participate in the Third International Summer School on Project Management, organized by a group of universities and hosted by the University of Nicosia. Although the software tool provides an option for users to develop their own scenarios and run the simulation tool to solve them, this option has not yet been incorporated into the curriculum.

A recurring theme in the feedback received from students was the value they assigned to their learning experience through the use of PTB. Some indicative testimonials are included. "This simulation made me understand the material of the course better than if I had studied for several continuous hours" pointed out an undergraduate student in an MIS major. A Computer Engineering major added "It is as if we are working in a real-life situation and we need to balance constraints to find a working solution". Overall, students were positive that the simulation helped them acquire knowledge in project management in a thorough and efficient way. Several students pointed out that the process of learning through simulation was more challenging and stimulating than the one followed in lecture-led settings.

Another theme in students' feedback was the relevance of the simulation training in their future professional endeavors. In the words of one graduate student, "I can see value in using this simulation because I feel reassured about the body of knowledge that I have acquired and on which I'll be tested to get professional certification. I can also see value even in those few cases where I make mistakes, because it is okay to do them here, learn and avoid them next time rather than learning them the hard way".

The PTB simulation-based learning environment not only addresses the cognitive requirements of a project management course, it also enhances the human aspects of Project Management. It provides an immersive environment for students to form a team, assign roles, negotiate different approaches, apply project management principles and techniques and learn, not only the project management-related issues, but also the process through which collaborative decision making can be achieved. As one student pointed out, "By now I have been involved in several team projects [in other courses]; they were all rather compartmentalized. I mean each one of us [team members] agreed to undertake a specific task and had minimum interaction with the rest of the team while completing it. At the end, each one of the team members would put our parts together and in most cases we would end up with a mash of distinctive parts instead of a coherent and complete project. In this [PTB] simulation, however, the whole team was required to work together all the time. I like that".

In conclusion, faculty members and students at the University of Nicosia see a strong value in the use of PTB simulation software in their project management courses. It enriches the learning experience of students in different dimensions. It enables them to visualize what their future professional experience will resemble, prepares them accordingly, and assists them to acquire authentic skills and knowledge. Students acknowledge that the use of project management simulation-based learning is challenging and engaging and allows them to learn in a secure, reassuring way.

9.5. EUROPE: Technical University of Munich

Rainer Kolisch, TUM School of Management, Technical University of Munich, Germany

9.5.1. *Outline of the course and the program*

The Project Team Builder (PTB, Shtub 2012) is used in the course "Project Management". This course is an elective in the third year of the undergraduate program, "Management and Technology," taught at the TUM

School of Management. The three-year program provides a curriculum that integrates management and technology with a focus towards quantitative and international studies; 70% of the courses are in business and 30% of the courses are in technology. Students acquire a good mix of management and technical capabilities. In the first three semesters, students have to take mandatory courses such as Mathematics, Statistics, Management Science, and Empirical Research, which provides students with a solid quantitative background. Due to the international orientation of the program, a significant number of exchange students participate for one or two semesters. These students are mainly from Business schools in Europe, and also from Asia and Australia. Of the 40 students taking the project management class, about 50% are German and 50% are international.

9.5.2. *The PTB-lecture and assignment*

After students have learned the fundamentals of a project, as well as the planning tasks of operational project management (time planning, cost planning, and resource planning), they are introduced to the project planning cycle. Emphasis is given to the fact that planning is not undertaken in a strict sequential process, but that there are loops and iterations which have to be undertaken. In this context, the multi-mode concept is introduced to the students showing them that there are often a number of ways an activity can be processed and that these ways impact the duration and the resource demand of the activities and the project. Finally, the notion of risk, which has been discussed in time planning with stochastic activity durations, is extended to the availability of resources.

Afterwards, the PTB is briefly introduced, using an introductory case as an example. The overall planning task, the different objectives, constraints and decisions are explained. Afterwards, details of the activities, the resources, costs and budget, quality and risk are explained. Key features of the PTB are shown by solving the case in class. Students are introduced to different graphical representations, such as activity networks, Gantt-charts and resource charts. Furthermore, the students are shown various types of constraint violations and how they can be resolved. Finally, the students are introduced to the risks which can unfold, how risks impact the solution, and what policies can be used to counter the risks.

As one of the course assignments, student teams solve independently the Radar Development scenario case that accompanies the student-version of the PTB software. Students have to hand in their scenario's summary report, which is generated by PTB after successfully solving the case.

9.5.3. *Students' response*

At the end of the course, students were asked to fill out a questionnaire regarding the use of PTB in the course; 53% of the students stated they would have liked to spend more time with PTB, 43% were pleased with the time spent with PTB, and 3% (one student) would have liked to spend less time with PTB. A number of students explicitly stated that working with PTB was fun.

9.5.3.1. *Takeaways when working with the PTB*

Students stated four main takeaways: First, they learned that the three basic planning tasks–schedule planning, cost planning, and resource planning, which had been treated in class, are interrelated and have to be done in an integrated fashion. Second, they learned the value of thinking a project through in its entirety and coming up with a sound baseline plan. Third, they learned about the devastating effects of risk, which altered activity durations and availability of resources and made plans obsolete. One aspect of this takeaway was that wrong decisions made in an early project phase can have severe consequences on the performance of the project or can even make the project fail. Fourth, the students learned about all aspects which had not been covered in depth in lectures, such as multiple modes, activity splitting, and setup time for altering the availability of resources, idle costs of resources, regular and subcontracted resources, quality, and lean criteria.

9.5.3.2. *Improved use of PTB in class*

Some students suggested that PTB should be used throughout the entire course and that they should be encouraged to create their own case rather than solving one of the existing cases. Another suggestion was to initially solve a case without PTB first, and then resolve using PTB. Some students proposed a closer alignment of the class content with the functionality of the PTB. Some students asked for more challenging cases. One student suggested using PTB at the beginning of the course in order to expose students to the difficult planning problems in project management early on and thus, invoke interest for the planning concepts taught throughout the course.

9.5.3.3. *Usefulness of PTB for planning real projects*

When asked about the usefulness of PTB for planning real projects, 70% of the students deemed PTB helpful for managing real projects. Some of the students addressed the problem of acquiring the required data. It became apparent that some students viewed PTB as software for planning projects in addition to being software for teaching Project Management.

9.6. ASIA: L&T Institute of Project Management, India

Hariharan Subramanyan, L&T Institute of Project Management, Mumbai, India

Simulations are often considered to be efficient for professionals' training. Experiential learning makes simulation a good pedagogical tool for educating working professionals. A study involving simulation-based training using the PTB software system was carried out at the L&T Institute of project management in India with 12 participants with real-world backgrounds in Transportation Infrastructure. Projects, in this field, generally involve road, rail, and runway construction. Team members had a range of years of business experience across a variety of business and engineering disciplines. The number of years of work experience varied from 5 to 25 years, and the functional areas of expertise included planning, procurement, site construction services, plant & machinery and business development. Team members had a good understanding of and experience with projects. Participants formed three teams and their experiences were recorded.

A good level of motivation and participation of team members was observed throughout the training process. This kind of learning environment is difficult to achieve in a typical classroom session and, hence, supports the idea that experiential learning is not just a desirable component in professional training, it is in fact essential. The course instructor observed the following tendencies as the student teams integrated and converted their learning into actions under real-time conditions:

- Teams scheduled their tasks as per the project documentation which provided only estimates of duration by the technical teams and, as a result, ended up with having no provision to accommodate time contingencies arising out of managerial decisions.
- Critical activities were identified in terms of schedule during the planning phase and participants realized that activities became critical in terms of resources in the execution phase.
- Mechanically assigning resources based on their availability or cost criteria did not ensure project delivery. Though theoretically one is correct in assigning resources that are available during a particular point in time, productivity may not be up to the mark. This may be attributed to factors, such as poor motivation of the resource.
- A project can suffer as resources are idle during a period in which activity was planned. In retrospect, some of the idle resources could have been deployed in alternative activities during the idle time.
- Participants were logical in sequencing their activities and using scheduling software. However, success in scheduling lies in allowing slack or buffer time which is not necessarily described in the project description, but could come up from brainstorming possible scenarios. None of the teams did this, and it resulted in teams performing poorly, as no provision for buffer time was kept. Although in theory the schedules were achievable, in reality the teams were not able to meet the schedule targets.
- Participants sought three important dimensions while participating in simulation-based training — Relevance, Reality, and Reliability (3 R's).

The PTB study makes evident that concept-based learning needs to be complemented with application-based simulation software. For example, conventional training emphasizes resource allocation with resource availability while simulation-based training allows participants to look at other dimensions, such as resource motivation and choice of make or buy decisions, thereby enhancing students' understanding of the intricacies and subtleties of Project Management.

Design and evaluation are complementary in developing a simulation training tool, and there should be sufficient scope for both academics and designers to continually evaluate a training tool for its relevance, reality and reliability. This synergy is enabled by a strong delivery and feedback mechanism between those who design and those who take the design forward in a classroom environment.

A good simulation training tool should have the following features:

- Sound theoretical concept orientation and discussion prior to simulation training.
  - PTB has a structured level of difficulty so that training can progress from a low level to a higher level of difficulty.
- Motivate and help project managers understand the knowledge and application requirements in a project and thereby connect hard and soft skills.
  - PTB meets this requirement in helping project personnel appreciate their knowledge application in a simulated environment.
- Both academic relevance and professional practice in terms of reliability embedded in a tool allow students to connect concepts to their projects and make the simulation more motivating (Relevance and Reliability).
  - Participants look for relevance to their business. PTB's scenario building facility aids in meeting this requirement.
- A simulation tool must have a provision to create more scenarios that suit the specific business environment of those undergoing training (Reality).
  - As the participants came from transportation and construction backgrounds, they preferred to develop project scenarios involving these disciplines. This learning experience was satisfied by the PTB Scenario Builder which allowed students to create projects with a transportation or construction theme.

In conclusion, integrating simulation-based training into a conventional project management course improves classroom participation. Theoretical sessions and lectures are effective, but incomplete if not complemented with experiential learning techniques. Students agreed that simulation-based training can contribute to the effectiveness in the learning experience and also opined that the effectiveness improves by having a provision to create more scenarios that suit their specific business environment.

Designers of simulation-based training should consider adding a simulation of behavioral aspects, conflict management, communication, human resources, stakeholder engagement, negotiations, and contract administration. Integration of these business skills, within a tool, such as the PTB which emphasizes the more technical aspects of project management such as scheduling and resource management, can strengthen the learning process and improve the effectiveness of the project management pedagogical process in the future.

9.7. Global International Course: Global Network for Advanced Management

Matthew O'Rourke, Yale School of Management, *USA*

Course taught by Avraham Shtub, Technion Israel Institute of Technology, *Israel*

9.7.1. *About the Global Network for Advanced Management*

Established in 2012, the Global Network for Advanced Management is comprised of 29 business schools from diverse regions, countries, cultures, and economies in different stages of development. The Network connects students, staff, faculty, and alumni of the schools to allow them to develop an understanding of the challenges, differences, and commonalities in their economies. The Network was designed as a shift away from the traditional one-to-one model for business school partnerships, instead, focusing on the comparative advantages of each member institution to address problems that are both complex and global in nature affecting a variety of sectors.

9.7.2. *About the New Product Development Course*

New Product Development (NPD) was one of the first courses offered as part of the Global Network for Advanced Management's online course offerings for students. The course is built around the idea that new products are a critical component, essential to the survival of and success of organizations. This course is designed to teach the tools and techniques developed to support the NPD process, offering students the opportunity to gain insight from case studies about successes and failures. The course also offers students a chance to implement the tools, techniques, and learnings from the course in a simulated environment.

The course uses simulation software to provide challenges involving resource management and timetables surrounding bringing a product to market. The simulator challenges students using practical management problems that business leader's face when attempting to develop a new product.

9.7.3. Class snapshot

Students participating in the class were from a diverse array of cultures, economic backgrounds, and work experiences. Students were from more than 15 countries, coming from a variety of career paths, including a materials sourcing strategist for companies in Mexico; a product manager for wearable smartwatches in Asia; a technology developer and engineer focused on software products in India; and a manager as part of a chemical company based in Asia selling goods to African suppliers.

9.7.4. Global virtual learning as part of new product development

Students for the Global Network for Advanced Management's small network online course met virtually each week to attend class sessions and conduct teamwork. The course "met" via the Canvas and Xoom digital platforms, where students gave presentations in real-time in a video-conference setting moderated by both a professor and a teaching assistant.

Early in the course, students were assigned to global virtual teams, with an aim of providing as much cultural diversity as possible while working through both the technical challenges of completing a project in real-time with deadlines. That challenge proved to have several real-world applications and barriers that students would face while working in a global environment. Chase Harmon, a Yale School of Management class of 2017 student, said that culture factors in when holding discussions with teammates, especially in how conversations are framed. Harmon said he ran into challenges in communicating clearly with his team when using the simulator. "I think more interactivity would be optimal for this...it's not very easy to be in the simulator all at once (as a team). Often, the project was me running the simulation, explaining all of the inputs I used, taking screenshots, and sending them to the team," he said.

An added benefit of the virtual classroom setting is the exposure to global ideas within a local context. Shiny Krishnan, a student at the Indian Institute of Technology Bangalore, said the collaborations and individual presentations from students allowed her to hear ideas from other teams as well, including an urban farming/gardening program and a bike share initiative that she thought could find success in India, too.

"Whether it was an aggregator or something else, I found some very relevant business ideas that could be applied to India," Krishnan said. "I like the fact that we worked globally from a virtual perspective and while it would have been easier to work with a team just in India, I would not have received the global experience that I did."

Another student said the gamification was a particularly useful asset as part of the overall experience, but felt that the project simulator should be adjusted for other situations, such as services. Reynaldo Vilchis, a student at EGADE Business School in Mexico, said his team's plans — an elderly care service facility — required more human resources versus natural resources, and thought that the simulator should have a component for services-based industries. "Beyond the simulator, in this type of class you're going to get to know at least three or four people in depth from several different cultures, including the professor, who has a much different approach than someone at my home business school. I think you learn from this type of format in a way that you're unable to with a traditional classroom."

Appendix

The Next Step — Creating and Managing Multiple Scenarios

A.1. Introduction

The student version of the Project Team Builder that accompanies this introductory level book is designed to expose the reader to the basic concepts, tools, and techniques of project management by integrating hands-on training with the traditional way of learning from textbooks. By deploying simulation-based training, we hope to help the reader gain a better understanding of the different knowledge areas of project management and their interaction with each other. The scenario selected for this book is simple and easy to understand, and, yet, it integrates the different project management aspects discussed in the book.

Simulation-based training is used in advanced project management courses as well. Multiple scenarios with increasing levels of difficulty can help the trainee build a better understanding of the impact of uncertainty and risk and develop the skill needed to cope with very tight constraints (resource constraints, due date constraints, and cash flow constraints). The full version of PTB comes with a library of easy, medium, and difficult scenarios. Furthermore, the Scenario Builder that comes with it can be used to develop new project scenarios.

In this appendix, we present an example of a final project done by a team of graduate students that had to develop a new scenario that applies project management methodologies and implements the techniques and

157

tools of project management discussed in the first eight chapters of this book by using the PTB simulator. The case study was developed by a team of students at the Technion — Israel Institute of Technology, under the guidance of the first author. The case involves the design, development, and construction of a power station and is based on a real-world project.

A.2. Student Project: Design, Development, and Construction of a Power Station

A.2.1. *Project background*

After several years of not building any new power stations, the power company needed to increase generation capacity which could be satisfied by the construction of additional power stations. The project, described in this case study, was actually the second phase of a larger, overall project. In Phase I, concluded in 2005, a gas turbine was constructed as an additional source of power in the country. Once the gas turbine was in place, it was economic and environmentally friendly to add a combined cycle unit to the gas turbine unit. A short company profile, including a summary of its existing power station infrastructure, is presented below:

A.2.2. *Company profile*

- The Company is a public and government-owned company;
- The Company's activities are generation, transmission and transformation, distribution, supply, and sale of electricity to all sectors in the economy;
- The Company owns and operates 17 power stations,
    - 18 steam-driven units,
    - 30 gas turbines, of which 14 are combined-cycle units;
- The Company's installed capacity stood at 13,617 MW;
- The Company employs 12,754 workers;
- The Company provides service to 2.63 million customers.

Power Stations:

- Coastal Stations
  — The generator is steam driven.
  — Operating on coal, natural gas, and oil.
- Inland Stations
- Gas Turbine:
  — The generator is hot-air driven.
  — Heavy-duty gas turbine.
  — Combined cycle gas turbines. Jet gas turbines — aviation jet engine.
  — Operating on natural gas and diesel fuel.

A.2.3. Stakeholder mapping and requirements

In Table A.1, the key stakeholders, including their level of influence and importance, are described. The needs and expectations of each group are also summarized, as well as their role and participation in the project team.

A.3. Life Cycle Cost

A Life Cycle Cost (LCC) analysis was performed in order to support the "GO/NO GO" decision for the project. It calculates the Net Present Value (NPV) over the project life cycle.

The project budget is allocated and approved by COMPANY management. Funding is derived from the COMPANY's total budget. The COMPANY's finance department monitors project expenses. Apart from the budget allocated for the project from the COMPANY's total budget, there are no other expected income sources during the power unit's construction. Incomes from the project will start only after the new unit is synchronized with the existing electricity network and begins to produce electricity.

Income depends on general electricity consumption and electricity rates that are set by the Electricity Authority. Additionally, rates vary by type of customer — domestic or industrial. The default rates are 40–45 cents for 1 KV h plus 14 NIS per month.

Table A.1.   Stakeholder mapping

#	Stakeholder	Definition	Influence	Priority	Needs, Expectations	Actions
1	Internal customer (Company)	Company's operating department	3	7	On-time delivery	Monitoring, receiving, updated reports
2	Project sponsor	The Government	10	10	Ongoing electricity supply and complying with regulations	Monitoring, receiving, updated reports
3	Product users	Electricity users	3	4	Ongoing electricity supply	None
4	Regulators	The electricity authority, Ministry of Environmental Protection	8	8	Set standards for pollution, safety, security, etc.	Monitoring
5	Subcontractors and suppliers	Subcontractors and suppliers	8	6	Achieving contracts and receiving on-time payments; Maximize orders and cash flow	Offering competitive bids and offering quality products & service
6	Competition	Private power stations and electricity manufacturers	3	1	Not adding new stations	Applying to the government to receive licenses for new stations
7	Project team members	Construction, design, and procurement department	6	8	On-time internal service and good communications	Meetings, reports, e-mails, and calls
8	Management	Board of directors and Company's CEO	9	10	On-time delivery and maintaining the budget	Monitoring, schedule, and budget

The following assumptions were made for the cost/benefit analysis:

- Average rate of 50 cents per KV h (including the constant rate per month).
- Total operating time is evaluated as 65% — the new unit will generate electricity on a regular basis apart from when the electricity load is low (for example, off-peak times) and when it is undergoing maintenance; scheduled maintenance is assumed to require 20% of capacity, and unscheduled maintenance due to equipment malfunctioning is estimated to be 15% of capacity.
- The additional unit will produce 100 MV. Therefore, its capacity per month is $100 \times 1,000 \times 24 \times 30 = 72,000,000$ KV h.
- The unit is expected to function for 30 years.
- Annual unit maintenance cost is estimated to be 5% of its original construction cost.
- Cost of fuel is not added to the cost, since the unit uses the waste heat from the gas turbine to make steam to generate additional electricity via a steam turbine and doesn't use any additional fuel.
- Miscellaneous costs, such as the cost of transmitting and connecting to customers were deemed to be minimal and ignored.

From Fig. A.1, the project returns a positive cash flow beginning in time period 8. The project NPV after eight years is −103.49M NIS. From that point on, a constant, annual profit is expected, and therefore the decision for the project is "GO".

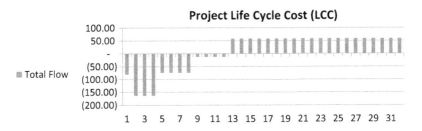

Fig. A.1. Project Life Cycle Cost

A.4. Alternative Selection

A.4.1. *Introduction*

In designing the new power unit, several design alternatives were considered. The alternatives were evaluated from the perspective of financial outcomes, available resource specialization, and total project lead time. The following alternatives were reviewed:

1. **Single-shaft vs. Multi-shaft systems**
   Single-shaft combined-cycle system:
   The gas turbine, steam turbine, and generator are installed in a tandem arrangement on a single shaft.
   Single-phase applications.

   Multi-shaft combined-cycle system:
   One or more gas turbine generators and HRSGs that supply steam through a common header to a separate single steam turbine generator unit.

2. **Procurement**
   One Procurement package (one vendor) versus separate packages for the major system.

3. **Vendors**
   Known Western vendors versus new Far East vendors.

A.4.2. *Alternative score method*

In order to evaluate these three decisions, a list of stakeholder requirements was delineated. Each requirement was ranked in importance from 1 to 5. The score of each alternative was then ranked with respect to each requirement on a scale of 1–10 based on the alternative's ability to satisfy the particular requirement. This scoring method is similar conceptually to the Analytical Hierarchy Process (AHP). A weighted score for each alternative is computed, see Table A.2.

A.4.3. *Result*

The best alternative for every criterion is shown and marked. In practice, the COMPANY chose multi-shaft systems, procurement in separate packages, and Western markets.

Table A.2. Scoring each alternative

Requirements	Importance	Shaft Systems		Procurement		Markets	
		Single Shaft	Multi Shaft	Package	Seperate Packages	Western Market	Far East Market
High Performance	5	8	9	9	9	9	7
Stay in Schedule	4	10	8	9	6	8	8
Stay in Budget	5	9	7	9	6	6	9
High Quality	4	9	7	8	7	8	6
High Durability	3	8	8	8	6	9	7
Preserving the Knowledge	5	8	8	6	10	8	8
High Reliability	4	10	9	8	7	9	7
Low Maintenance Cost	3	8	7	7	9	7	9
Low Required Human Resource	3	9	6	9	7	7	8
Closeness to Supplier	2	9	9	9	9	9	6
Known Methods of Work	4	8	9	9	9	10	6
Score		87.14	79.29	82.38	77.38	81.43	74.29
Normalized Score		0.87	0.79	0.82	0.77	0.81	0.74

A.5. Project Scope

A.5.1. *The project goal*

To construct a multi-shaft power generating system, procured from several Western vendors in separate contracts.

A.5.2. *Statement of work (SOW)*

An outline of the COMPANY's Statement of Work (SOW) is presented in this section. The SOW defines project scope, including key deliverables of each phase, project cost, and project schedule.

A.5.2.1. *Applicable documents*

List of applicable customer specifications and procedures:

- Technical specifications for the power plant multi-shaft combined cycle power station (mechanical and electrical).
- Civil engineering specification.
- Quality assurance procedure.
- Safety specification.

List of applicable standards:

- ISO 9001:2008

A.5.2.2. *Design*

The design includes the following activities:

- Drawings of the new additional unit.
- Calculations and analyses of the design.
- Procedures & instructions.
- Reports & lists.
- Vendor documents.
- Purchase specification.
- Design criteria.
- Design change documents.

A.5.2.3. *Licensing*

Licensing includes procuring a license to build a new power station, a construction license, and an environmental license.

A.5.2.4. *Purchasing*

Purchasing includes:

- RFI-request for information.
- RFQ-request for quotation.
- Receiving and comparing quotations.
- Choosing and approving selected suppliers (a role of the purchasing committee).
- Signing purchasing agreements.
- Monitoring suppliers.

A.5.2.5. *Construction*

Construction includes civil engineering activities, such as cement work, building work, fencing, and sewage.

A.5.2.6. *Mechanical work*

Mechanical work includes assembling the additional unit, testing of the unit, wire laying, and fulfilling safety requirements.

A.5.2.7. *Electrical work*

Electrical work includes wire laying, wiring, and control panel assembly.

A.5.2.8. *Launching*

Launching includes cold tests, hot tests, synchronization, and commercial launch.

A.5.3. *WBS*

A Work Breakdown Structure (WBS) is depicted in Fig. A.2.

The WBS was established by the planning department and approved by the project administration committee.

A.6. Organizational Breakdown Structure (OBS)

The COMPANY's Organizational Breakdown Structure (OBS) is functional, as seen below in Fig. A.3.

Both the WBS and OBS are functional and, hence, they are compatible.

A.7. Communications Management and Leadership

A.7.1. *Communication*

Communication is broken down as follows:

- Monthly reports of the project manager.

  The project manager is required to submit a monthly report to the VP which includes:

  — Schedule control
  — Budget control
  — Procurement control
  — Statutory control

- Managing an event journey.

  The project manager is required to document events that occur in the project in order to:

  — Use the information for decision making.
  — Use the information as a reliable database for organizational learning.

- Weekly meetings of the Project Administration Committee.
- Informal communication based on conversations between team members of the different units.

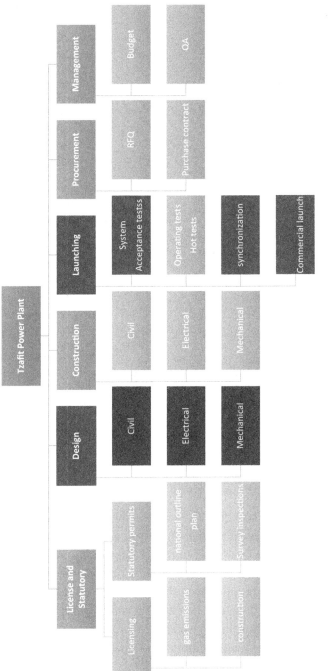

Fig. A.2. WBS

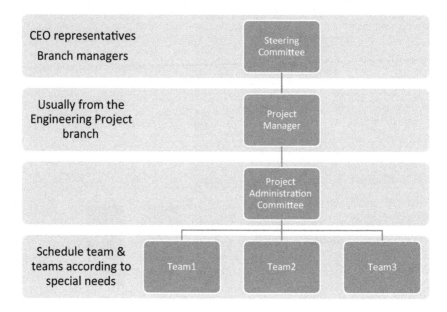

Fig. A.3. OBS

Fig. A.4. Project manager's span of responsibility

A.7.2. *Project manager's responsibilities*

The project manager coordinates activities and communications across the various internal organizational functions as well as externally with consultants and subcontractors. Figure A.4 depicts the project manager's span of responsibility. The project manager is responsible for dealing with uncertainties and integrating project modules between the various technical departments, such as design, purchasing, and construction. Finally, the project manager is responsible for conflict resolution, as disputes inevitably arise among project team members.

A.7.3. *Responsibilities and role description*

Roles and responsibilities should be defined and assigned to a work package in the WBS. The project manager prepares a formal LRC matrix at the beginning of the project. For example, the License and Statutory Work unit should be under the responsibility of the License and Permits Manager, as shown in Fig. A.5.

The LRC Matrix:

Work Packages	Project Manager	Design Engineer Manager	Construction Site Manager	Schedule Manager	Budget Manager	License and Permits Manager	Procurement Manager	Synchronization Manager
Licensing	5	2	2	5	5	1	2	2
Design	5	1	2	5	5	2	2	2
Construction	5	2	1	4	4	3	3	2
Launching	5	4	4	5	5	2	4	1
Procurement	5	4	2	5	5	2	1	2
Management	1	3	3	3	3	3	3	3

1 - Prime responsibility
2 - May be notified
3 - Must be consulted
4 - May be consulted
5 - Must be notified
6- Approval

Fig. A.5. LRC matrix to assign roles and responsibilities to each manager involved in the project

A.8. Labor Estimation and Duration

Each manager who was responsible for a particular work package was asked to estimate the work needed to complete their assigned activities. Table A.3 presents the durations estimated for each activity and immediate predecessors. Each period consists of two months. The duration times are assumed to be stochastic, and an optimistic, pessimistic, and most likely duration time is given for each activity.

Table A.3. Estimates of time durations and predecessors for each activity

Activity	Immediate Predecessors	Mode	Optimistic	Likely Duration	Pessimistic Duration
A Procurement	—	A	6	7	8
		B	5	6	7
		C	7	8	9
B License for construction	A	A	3	4	5
C License for electrical building	A	A	1	2	3
D Foundations for boiler and chimney	C	A	1	2	3
		B	2	3	3
		C	1	1	1
E Boiler and chimney installation	D	A	3	4	5
		B	4	5	6
		C	2	3	4
F Foundations for turbine	B	A	2	3	4
		B	3	4	5
		C	2	3	4
G Turbine installation	F	A	1	2	3
		B	2	3	4
		C	1	1	1
H Foundations for condenser and cooler systems	A	A	1	2	3
		B	2	3	4
		C	1	1	1

I	Condenser and cooler installation	H	A	3	4	5
			B	4	5	6
			C	2	3	4
J	Foundations for pipe and pump systems	B	A	1	1	2
			B	1	2	3
			C	1	1	1
K	Pipe and pump systems installation	J	A	1	2	3
			B	2	3	4
L	Foundation and construction of electrical building	C	A	5	6	7
			B	6	7	8
			C	4	5	6
M	System control installation	L	A	1	2	3
			B	2	3	4
			C	1	1	1
N	Electricity final test	M	A	1	2	3
			B	1	1	1
O	Launching	P, H, I,K,N,M	A	1	2	3
			B	1	1	1
			C	2	3	4
P	Cleaning and test	E	A	1	2	3
			B	1	1	1

A.9. Project Scheduling

In order to evaluate the probability of finishing the project on time, a Monte Carlo simulation was performed using the PTB simulator. The simulation results for 10,000 runs are given below in Fig. A.6:

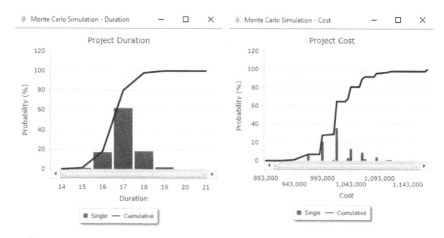

Fig. A.6. Monte Carlo simulation to estimate the probability of finishing on time

Based on the results of the simulation, the project will be completed by time period 17 with a probability of 80%. The project is guaranteed to finish by time period 19. The associated Gantt chart is given in Fig. A.7, and the network is given in Fig. A.8.

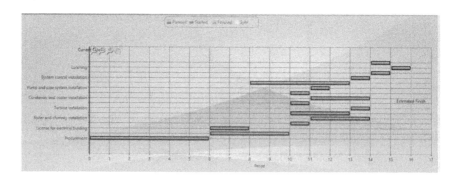

Fig. A.7. Gantt chart

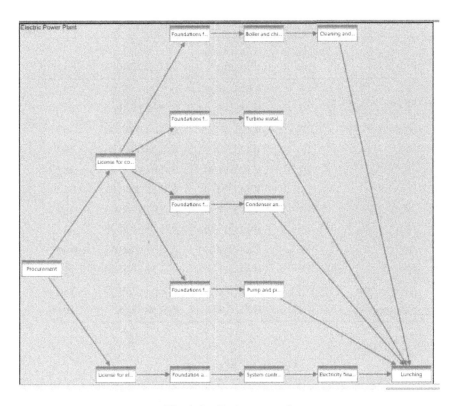

Fig. A.8. Project network

Table A.4 illustrates ten runs of the simulation.

A.10. Resource Information

Table A.5 provides a snapshot of resource usage, as generated by the PTB.

A.10.1. *Human resources in the company*

Engineers are the most expensive resource (labor). In scheduling resources, the users attempted to smooth out demand for each type of resource in order to minimize workforce fluctuations and reduce peak demand. A smooth demand schedule leads to avoidance of costs associated with hiring and firing workers.

Table A.4.   10 runs of the simulation

#	Simulation Time	Simulation Cash	Total Cost	Benefit
1	17	₪ 707,265.00	₪ 3,358,440.00	98.12
2	19	₪ 458,355.00	₪ 3,606,940.00	98.12
3	17	₪ 422,715.00	₪ 3,643,440.00	98.12
4	18	₪ 125,315.00	₪ 3,941,940.00	98.12
5	20	₪ 12,540.00	₪ 4,048,440.00	98.12
6	19	₪ 247,990.00	₪ 3,817,940.00	98.12
7	18	₪ 452,140.00	₪ 3,613,940.00	98.12
8	17	₪ 433,980.00	₪ 3,631,440.00	98.12
9	17	₪ 547,890.00	₪ 3,517,940.00	98.12
10	17	₪ 348,995.00	₪ 3,716,940.00	98.12
Average	17.9	₪ 375,718.50	₪ 3,689,740.00	98.12
Std. deviation	1.12	₪ 214,188.41	₪ 213,448.68	0.00

Table A.5.   Resource usage

Human Resource	Cost per Period (NIS)	Idle Cost (Period) (NIS)	Availability (%)	Releasing/ Assigning Cost (NIS)	Releasing/ Assigning Lead Time (weeks)
Engineer	12,000	6,000	95	100/100	1
Technician	8,000	4,000	92	75/75	1
Worker	5,000	2,500	90	50/50	1

A.10.2.   *External and fixed cost resources*

The COMPANY mostly uses external subcontractors for civil engineering work such as construction and installation of the boiler and chimney, as well as construction and installation of turbines. Lifting & transporting equipment is also rented from outside suppliers on an as-needed basis. A complete list of subcontractors is given in Table A.6.

Table A.6. List of subcontractors

Task Name	Task Status	Selected Mode	Planned Duration	Actual Duration	Planned Cost	Actual Cost
				Cost Schedule Control Electric Company		
Procurement	Planned	Supplier B	6	0	366000	0
License for construction	Planned	Unique way	4	0	337600	0
License for electrical building	Planned	Unique way	2	0	169600	0
Foundations for boiler and chimney	Planned	Subcontractor	1	0	57100	0
Boiler and chimney installation	Planned	Subcontractor	3	0	338000	0
Foundations for turbine	Planned	Supplier A	3	0	161100	0
Turbine installation	Planned	Subcontractor	1	0	116310	0
Foundations for condenser and cooler system	Planned	Subcontractor	1	0	58100	0
Condenser and cooler installation	Planned	Subcontractor	3	0	338310	0
Foundations for pipe and pump system	Planned	Supplier A	1	0	55100	0
Pump and pipe system installation	Planned	Supplier A	2	0	225310	0
Foundations for construction of electrical building	Planned	Subcontractor	5	0	269100	0
System control installation	Planned	Subcontractor	1	0	117310	0
Electricity final test	Planned	High-Quality	2	0	115000	0
Lunching	Planned	Fast	1	0	83500	0
Cleaning and test	Planned	Low-Quality	1	0	43500	0

A.11. Budgeting

The PTB generates various financial reports including a period-by-period cash flow, as depicted in Table A.7. The planning budget for the project is shown in Table A.8. This budget was created by the project management team, in concert with key stakeholders, using the LCC methodology. Preparation of the planning budget for the project is an activity that is exogenous to the PTB platform.

A.12. Risk Management

As stressed throughout the text, a key role of the project manager is to manage risks. Each potential risk must be identified, including its probability

Table A.7. Period-by-period cash flow

	Budget Control Electic Company					
Period	Planned Cost	Actual Cost	Planned Income	Actual Income	Planned Total	Actual Total
1	131500	0	0	0	−131500	0
2	89500	0	0	0	−89500	0
3	89500	0	0	0	−89500	0
4	89500	0	0	0	−89500	0
5	89500	0	0	0	−89500	0
6	89500	0	47090	0	−42410	0
7	203700	0	0	0	−203700	0
8	200500	0	3000000	0	2799500	0
9	153100	0	0	0	−153100	0
10	149000	0	1600	0	−147400	0
11	278400	0	6300	0	−272100	0
12	452620	0	0	0	−452620	0
13	439000	0	7510	0	−431490	0
14	461620	0	12930	0	−448690	0
15	127000	0	500	0	−126500	0
16	91000	0	1000	0	−90000	0
17	109000	0	500	0	−108500	0

Table A.8. Project budget

Element		Cost (Million NIS)	Notes
Design		73.4	
Purchasing		470.9	
Construction	Internal Human Resource	165	
	Subcontractors	104	
	Total	269	
Synchronization	Internal Human Resource	20.4	
	Subcontractors	4.7	
	Total	25.2	
Others		81.6	
Total nominal cost		920	
Budget goal (target cost on simulation)		920	
Total budget		984.3	64.3 Management reserve
Total bid offer		1,000	

of occurrence. For each potential risk event, an approach and strategy for dealing with the risk event should, ideally, be defined in advance. A delineation of potential risks associated with the new power unit is given in Table A.9. The project management team also identified tactics for handling each risk event.

A.13. Running the Simulation

The project scenario was simulated using the PTB simulator. The results of 10 simulation runs are summarized in Table A.10. The average project duration is 17.9 and the average project cost is NIS 3.689 MM.

Table A.9. Risk event profile

| Risk Event | Impact | | | Probability of Occurring — on a Scale of 1–5 (5 is Highest) | Risk Dealing Approach | Treatment |
	Schedule	Benefit/ Performance	Budget			
Delay in obtaining licenses for electrical building	+	+	+	5	Avoidance	Separating the activity of obtaining the construction licenses into two different activities.
Lack of human resources		+		2	Mitigation	Creating a detailed schedule in order to use multi-project management and use resources effectively.
Early supply		+	+	4	Mitigation	Using a bigger area for organizing and building and applying just-in-time supply
Steel structure supply delay	+		+	1	Mitigation	• Adding more shifts. • Pre-assembly of other activities (such as piping) at a different place.
Low-pressure turbine discrepancy	+	+		2	Mitigation	Controlling the production and assembly
Conveying excessive cargo on-time coordination	+			4	Acceptance	Working with the police in order to coordinate an earlier police escort

Table A.10. The results of 10 simulation runs

Simulation Run	Project Duration	Project Cost
1	17	₪ 3.358,440.00
2	19	₪ 3.606,940.00
3	17	₪ 3.643,440.00
4	18	₪ 3,941,940.00
5	20	₪ 4,048,440.00
6	19	₪ 3,817,940.00
7	18	₪ 3,613,940.00
8	17	₪ 3,631,440.00
9	17	₪ 3,517,940.00
10	17	₪ 3,716,940.00
Average	17.9	₪ 3,689,740.00
Std. deviation	1,118033989	₪ 213,448.68